Answer Coming Soon

By the same author:

BLAMING NO ONE: Blog postings on arts, letters, policy
(New Academia Publishing/VELLUM Books, 2012)

Answer Coming Soon

More Blog Postings on Arts, Letters, Policy

Dan Whitman

Washington, DC

Copyright © 2016 by Dan Whitman
New Academia Publishing 2017

All rights reserved. No part of this book may be reproduced or transmitted in any form or by any means, electronic or mechanical, including photocopying, recording, or by any information storage and retrieval system.

Printed in the United States of America

Library of Congress Control Number: 2017930347
ISBN 978-0-9981477-6-5 paperback (alk. paper)

 An imprint of New Academia Publishing

New Academia Publishing
4401-A Connecticut Ave. NW, #236, Washington DC 20008
info@newacademia.com - www.newacademia.com

Cover photo (and page 218), courtesy of the photographer David Montgomery.
Photos on pages 12, 14, 18, 21, 42, 47, 50, 71, 105, 118, 134, 161, 187, 202, 213-14, 217, 220, 24, and 237, courtesy of the author.
Photo on page 111, http://www.trykkefrihed.dk. All efforts have been made to contact a possible rights holder.
All other photos are from Creative Commons.

Contents

Introduction: Minding Your Business	1
Francophobia in Retreat	5
Where is Philippe Markington? (Part One)	9
Where is Philippe Markington? (Part Two)	14
"Interrogatoire" (Part Three)	18
But Where is Markington? (Part Four)	21
Reading from Africa	25
Turf Issues	29
An Overnight in Mainz	33
The Dog is Well	38
Vladimir	42
And a Third Russian	47
Emperors' Clothes	50
Inauguration Transfiguration	53
Remembering Todman	56
Thought's Colors	60
Believing is Seeing	64
A Class Act from Bangui	68
Safety in Numbers	71
Gone but Not Forgotten	75
Ward Just and *American Romantic*	78
Woman in the Dunes	82
Sandra's Moment (Part One)	86
Sun Tzu in a Cubicle (Part Two)	89

Not Funny Any More	93
This Happened March 20, and It Could Happen to You	97
Faulkner Trending	101
Small Enough to Succeed	105
Looking Before You Leap	108
Bronx Cheer for a Danish Court	111
Saved by a Tux	115
Not Taking Sides Yet	118
My Three Weapons	122
Voice of… Reason	126
Sometimes He Wondered	129
There They Go Again	134
Overnight to Ystad	137
Ruthless	142
The Great James Baker	145
Cable to Nowhere	148
Potato, Potahto, Monogamy, Polygamy	152
Homicide Fine, Fax Not So Good	154
"Mister Bratton, I Presume?"	157
"Je m'en vais"	161
Revenge of the Clowns	165
An Appreciation of Pat Nixon	169
The Man No One Would Be	173
A Cure Worse than the Disease	177
Keeping the Memory	181
Haiti's Amazing Language	184
The Center Folds	187
Old Wine, New Battles	191
You Say Boots, I Say Rubbers	195
The Old Block	198
Late Lunch	202

Answer Coming Soon	206
Finding Common Ground with Lester	210
While I Was Out of Town	213
Trash Tree in Malabo	217
Walking Dschang	220
Restless	224
Ambassador to the Mountain	228
Managing Information Technology for a New Us	233
Uh Oh, Nativism is Not Only Offensive	237
Arounothay's Tux	240
Why I Learned French	244
Kindly Make Sense of This	247
Linear Thinking	251
Village Fool	256

Introduction

Minding Your Business

One crisp, fall day in 1989, Secretary of State James Baker gave a short press conference in Copenhagen, maybe the shortest ever. The briefing papers had gone to him from our embassy, but something had gotten lost or overlooked; when a journalist asked him about nuclear ship visits (the main sticking point in our bilateral relationship), he went blank. A chorus of "Thank you Mister Secretary"s ended the whole ordeal within about 35 seconds of the start. The next time he came, a year later, he was prepped and ready.

Irony—the introduction of the unexpected in a series of predictable events or patterns—is the working element in comedy, tragedy, art, and music. The patterns neither get nor deserve much interest, while the interruptions do. Foreign policy dreads irony, but endures it all the time.

That is the texture of these blog postings. They follow an earlier collection, *Blaming No One*.

I was going to call this series "Dining with Murderers," but that was a bit *tiré par les cheveux*. What I had in mind was the life-sucking evenings around the table with people we never liked much. Ambassadors suffer these evenings the most; the rest of us in the Foreign Service get a taste, which instructs us to avoid high positions if we have our wits about us.

Ambassadors represent sovereigns (presidents, kings, dictators). This becomes an outmoded concept in an age where digital communication restricts—does not liberate—freedom of expression from the highest levels of government and business.

Think of it this way: Ambassador Chipski meets with key local contacts. Some represent or lend intellectual ferment, but 73.9 per cent are likely to be boring. The guests—bad, good, indifferent—find themselves at his table, alongside the occasional murderer. By this I mean those who harm their own communities. If you widen the definition to include the latter, you get up to the 85 per cent range. No footnote here because of course I'm faking it.

But these dinners can be lonely and enervating affairs, and can go long into the night, leaving the ambassador and colleagues dispirited and sleep-deprived. I saw one once (the hostess!) slumped forward over her own couch like a Stravinsky puppet, softly snoring through a tedious monologue by her Brazilian counterpart. How I admired and respected her! How I pitied her!

At my own lower level as public affairs officer, refilling wine glasses usually gave little joy. On a few occasions, days later someone would say, "You had So-and-So to your *house*? Really, for a meal? You mean the one who murdered five of his workers with his bare hands? Or was it the brother, who copped a plea and got to walk home after the indictment was lifted?" This was an actual case, not something I have made up here to spice an argument.

Compassion, please, for those who subject themselves to this form of toil, and the many more who fancy doing so, but never make it through the vetting process to land these coveted positions.

Diplomacy is a noble and energizing adventure, but the evenings – the evenings!

George F. Kennan, who got seventy percent of his things right and helped us make it through the Cold War, said this:

> The Foreign Service... can so easily become an unhealthy mode of life – unhealthy in the sheer physical and nervous sense. It does involve, and always will involve an intensity of social entertainment which goes far beyond what the human form, and in particular the human gastro-intestinal tract, was never meant to endure.
>
> ...They have eaten one too many a diplomatic dinner. They have pumped one too many a hand. They have exhausted the capacity for spontaneity. Let us not be superior! We all face these dangers—and some of us sooner than we like to think—and it will take our best efforts to avoid them.
> [*Foreign Service Journal*, May 1961]

The Foreign Service is one leg of this three-legged stool. Great practitioners are not lacking, but there is more. What choice do we have but to crowd onto the shoulders of our predecessors? Those who threaten to retreat to holographic traces merit full attention. The great ones break patterns and startle. The latter is what we live by, reminds us that we live.

In the chapters ahead, my questions, my answers appear to me like unfired clay. The binary human brain requires dialogue, Q&A. I enter the stream, do not originate or resolve it. The great Colman McCarthy said, "Do not answer the questions. Question the answers." By this he meant, do not be intellectually supine. To me the phrase means, "Keep the conversation going."

Acknowledgments to Tod Didier and Punditwire.com, where these pieces were first posted. And to David Montgomery for the cover photo.

As always I thank and acknowledge those who have encouraged and helped me on this particular project, including Tracy Denholm, Asuncion Sanz, Harvey Sachs, Kari Jaksa, Taya Louise Owens, Silke Schoch, Bettina Falsen, Katja Hering, Anita Lum, Dan Neher, Ilya Levin, June and Michael von Essen, Amparo Dalda, Bob LaGamma, Adela Momo-Boloso, Vladimir Pimonov, Rafal Najaat, Penny

Akahloun, Lelysaveta Schchepetylnykova, Joe Eldridge, Colman McCarthy, Fanta Aw, Mihailo Savic, Tanya Lafichenko, Sarith Sok, Manny Berard, George Ayitteh, Tierno Bah, Myra Michele Brown, Greg Garland, Taiyi Sun, Ed Kemp, Emily Cassano, Caryl Morris, Susan Golden, Dan Freeman, Jake Plevelich, Anna Lawton, Amitai Etzioni, Nicole Peacock, the late Mike Norton, Edwin Honig, and Calderón de la Barca.

Now to the anecdotes. As before, we recall the late Verlin Cassill saying, "All wisdom is contained in stories."

Francophobia in Retreat

June 17, 2012

To decipher the arcana, we used to tell students, "The World Bank is the one that messes up the economies of poorer countries, the International Monetary Fund for richer countries.

The dictum is now outworn, as should be any lingering bitter-ender Francophobia these days, with the remarkable Christine Lagarde now heading the IMF. Francophobia met strong headwinds June 12, at her presentation at the Center for Global Development (CGD) in Washington.

The managing director spoke to an audience of 200 and conversed on mic with CGD's founder, the redoubtable Nancy Birdsall, herself a former senior official in the InterAmerican Development Bank.

Lagarde understands the IMF's needs for informed friends. Her impressive ability to win them over puts the Fund in one of its finest moments so far.

As former finance minister of France, Lagarde knows about fiscal reform, monetary policy, tax incentives, stimulus… But she said up front that these were all short-term items in a classical toolbox, and that long-term development was her main interest. More intriguingly, as former agriculture minister as well, she sees beyond money alone. The innovation was to see the IMF in tandem with a larger development community, rather than the lever of one-armed bandits of cash transfers in emergency situations only.

"I'm not here to talk about the Euro crisis," she said. It was a moment of welcome humility, underscoring that the IMF can inform, guide, direct, coach, but can't fix big cash crises by itself, or just with money.

"It's true that the Eurozone is the epicenter of the problem, but the crisis is much wider."

Rationed bits of humor emphasized the point: when the Reuters correspondent asked if the IMF would bring any "pledges" to the Rio + 20 meeting next week, she paused and said, "Well, I'm only the managing director of the IMF." (The French artfully put negative concepts in affirmative turns of phrase, and vice versa.) Bottom line: the World Bank donates, the IMF calibrates. "I wish I were in that business [donations] but I'm not," she said.

Then she got to her business. "The poor suffer when the rich make the wrong decisions." Imagine: hurting the poor financially hurts us all. No touchy-feely here.

"Les pollueurs sont les payeurs," she said in the sole phrase uttered in her native language. ["The polluters should be those who pay."] Here we approach the core of her thinking: finance, labor, and environment can no longer be disaggregated. If they ever functioned as independent units, they are now fully intertwined. This point is not mere rhetoric, I think, but a way of turning traditional and worn developmental models on their head. Hence, the need for friendships and alliances with governments, but also with the International Labor Organization, non-profits like CGD, environmentalists, and others who can succeed only through teamwork.

"I'm not trying to remake the IMF as an environmental organization, but this issue is more important than the Euro crisis."

With Gallic insistence, challenging some pretty big names, Lagarde sees stimulus as a reductionist notion: "Not stimulus alone. We must rekindle demand."

The French provide ideas that are hard or sometimes impossible to implement (viz., the Declaration of the Rights of Man!), but without these admittedly cerebral frameworks, where would we be?

Identify problem, state goals. This simple practice eludes governments and practitioners, and yields disappointments from well-intentioned world-menders.

"We need to get the green economy right," she says, apologizing even for using the charged word "green." The calculating eye notes that the region in the world which least produces pollution (Africa) is the one to suffer most from its effects, through drought, flooding, and low crop yields. Thinking of this dispassionately, as a broken machine, might just lead to reversing the dysfunction.

Lagarde was coy and even hilarious in evading questions about U.S. domestic politics or even policy. Few whack-a-mole players get it better. She never said, "I don't speak about U.S. domestic politics"—she just plain doesn't.

She was equally charming in taking a young graduate student's question about IMF assistance to entities other than countries, for example, cities, states, and provinces which make efforts to break out of stagnation on environmental policy. She wrote the idea down, and said, "In fact I never thought of that. It will be on my to-do list." Home run for the grad student, likewise Lagarde.

Here is the notion Lagarde wanted most to drive home: something called "Getting the Price Right." She defined this concept by saying, "The harm we do would be reflected in the price we pay." Hence, fuel consumption, water use, dipping into resources should be calibrated and restored by the user to the common—and shrinking—pool available to others. There is nothing punitive in this, but it is a bold proposal to calculate the price of what we use and waste. This could come through direct taxes, cap and trade, carbon pricing, or any other way you want to work it. As she said, "You break it, you buy it."

The pricing and measuring of natural resources: if the IMF did nothing else, this alone would be the invention of a new approach to value and basic human relationships.

The occasion was the publication of an IMF report at midnight of June 11-12, now on its website. Lagarde hadn't had time to read the whole thing overnight. But Birdsall had. That's where the teamwork comes in.

Where is Philippe Markington? (Part One)

July 30, 2012

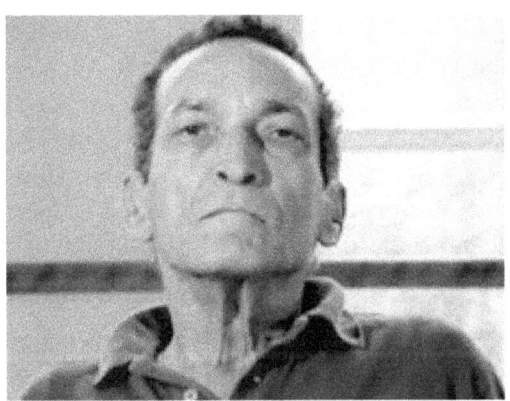

[Part one of four] On April 3, 2000, Haitian journalist Jean Léopold Dominique was shot dead in an ambush at his own radio station (Radio Haiti-Inter) on the Rue Delmas in Port-au-Prince. Maybe coincidentally, former and future president Jean-Bertrand Aristide flew to Miami the next day.

The date resonates in Haitian history as does November 22, 1963, in the United States. In a "Talk of the Town" piece in *The New Yorker* of April 20, long-time Aristide apologist Amy Wilentz described Dominique as "Haiti's JFK and Walter Cronkite."

I had tangled with the crotchety Dominique myself two months before, when as U.S. Embassy spokesman I had accepted his invitation for a live interview on his morning program "Face à la Nation." The bitter, brilliant Dominique had real and imagined issues with the United States, where he had taken refuge during the Duvalier and military regimes years earlier. He'd been a staunch supporter of Aristide after the latter's return to power in 1994. Like many others, Dominique repatriated himself at this earlier, auspicious time.

Dominique was no one's lapdog, however, and publicly criticized Aristide the first weekend of April 2000, for "surrounding yourself with filth." Haitians knew this referred to the drug and contraband trade among the president's subordinates. Seventy-two hours later, Dominique was dead.

Dominique maintained his credibility and the public's trust by having no real friends. He had lit into me February 8 for hypocrisy in U.S. policy toward Haiti, but then lightened up by the end of the hour when he seemed to take a liking to me. I'd met him once before (he had begged me in private not to "resist the galloping horse" of Aristide and his entourage, which he said was Haiti's future. He made very dramatic gestures with his expansive arms, leaning toward me and indicating his human version of a galloping horse).

Jonathan Demme's movie *The Agronomist* some years later looked into the nature of the country's leaders' backgrounds in agronomy, and the importance of the land in the people's identity. Dominique had made the same point to me during our conversation. It all sounded like Masonic gobbledygook to me, but Demme did nail the character and spirit of Dominique when he called him "a composite of Edward R. Murrow and Paul Revere."

Dominique knew he was skating on thin ice, and realized daggers were drawn on him. As early as October 18, 1999, he had said on the air that he thought drug kingpin and Haitian senator Dany Toussaint might want him dead. In his defiant (and eerily prophetic) public response, Dominique said, "If I am still alive, I will close down the station after having denounced the plot hatched against me and I will return into exile one more time with my wife and children." In a retrospective of his early sense of betrayal, he continued, "In 1991, I told Jean-Bertrand Aristide and René Préval [Haiti's president in 2000] to watch out for Cédras [the military leader who overthrew Aristide in 1992]. Titid said, 'Cédras and I are married!' One sad marriage!" ("Titid" was Aristide's public and affectionate nickname.)

Then with one of his marvelous classical flourishes, Dominique ended his October 18, 1999, broadcast, "Earlier I quoted another free man [Choderlos de Laclos, author of *Dangerous Relations*]. I end with Shakespeare: "The truth makes the Devil blush."

I guess Dominique liked his 2/8/00 interview with me, because he kept airing and re-airing it over the following days and weeks. Shortly before his assassination he put it on the air repeatedly – some said he knew he was in the regime's crosshairs, and wanted the implied protection of the U.S. Embassy he had so often vilified on his show. The day of his assassination, April 3, *Radio Haiti-Inter* broadcast the interview over ten times.

People are popped all the time in Haiti. In this case, for a few weeks things went fine for the poppers—until the international community got hold of the story and called repeatedly for "justice, and an investigation." Someone in Port-au-Prince had underestimated Dominique's prestige outside his own country.

As Jean Jean-Pierre said in *The Village Voice* April 18, "Dominique gained prominence in 1973 when U.S. ambassador and Duvalier apologist Clinton Knox was kidnapped by a group of leftists… Dominique's nonstop reportage and the subsequent cave-in of Baby Doc emboldened journalists and activists. Dominique's work…laid the foundations for an independent press in Haiti."

The April 3 affair gained in prominence, with the Inter-American Press Agency and Reporters sans Frontières calling for clarity. By April 25 a petition demanding a "timely response" from the government was signed by Richard Gere, Robert Redford, Jonathan Demme, Taylor Branch, Spalding Gray, Robert De Niro, Spike Lee, Paul Newman, Woody Allen, Edwidge Danticat, Harold Pinter, Martin Scorsese, Toni Morrison, Norman Mailer, Nora Ephron, Amy Wilentz, Denzel Washington, William Styron, Katherine Dunham, Gregory Peck, Paul Farmer, Lauren Bacall, Kenneth Starr, David Dinkins, and 184 others.

Uh-oh! Not the quiet removal of the pre-Internet era. Too many observers in the amphitheater this time.

Someone had to come up with something to explain Dominique's death, notwithstanding the state funeral in the national stadium

April 8, the highest pomp ever accorded a non-head of state in Haiti. Deflecting and refracting attention was indicated.

Meanwhile, the Haitian National Police (HNP) had some, mmmm, reshuffles. April 24, HNP Inspector General Luc Euchère Joseph slipped out of the country and made it to Switzerland. May 26, the HNP spokesman turned himself into the U.S. Embassy and asked for political asylum (he didn't get it).

The bizarre and louche Philippe Markington (identified as "engineer" on his ID cards) had begun visiting me in my office earlier in the year, and on April 24 handed me a handwritten, supposed "hit list" with names he said Aristide's Lavalas party was planning to knock off in the near future. He never asked for money or services in return, and I never gave him any. I said that as Public Affairs Officer in the embassy, I had no interest in corridor plots or hocus-pocus, but he left the list with me anyway.

Markington said he was with something called "The Aristide Foundation," and said he was appalled at what it had turned into. If true, this was a praiseworthy change of heart, but you never know. I offered him a public forum if he wanted to say something to the press, but he declined. I asked my embassy colleagues what to do, and they said, "Keep the contact; it's the only one we have."

So I did, until June 24, when my phone rang at home early on a Saturday morning. That would be the next segment of our little potboiler.

Where is Philippe Markington? (Part Two)
August 1, 2012

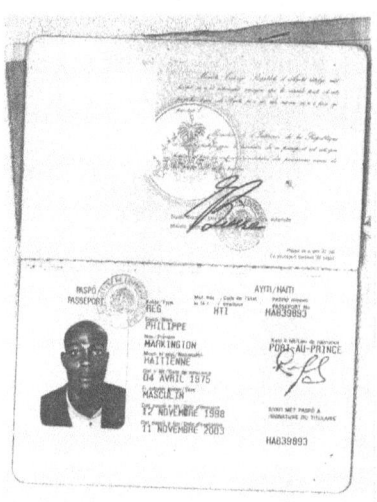

[Part two of four] If I said, "Markington dressed like a pimp," I would mean no disrespect to him or to pimps. He wore heavy, black, wool turtlenecks in the 90-degree heat, and a chest medallion that looked something like an Aztec calendar. He had the wandering eyes of a cocaine user, but I don't mean to draw conclusions here.

I had his phone number but never used it. I took his calls and allowed him to visit my office not for the pleasure of it, but because my embassy asked me to do so. His ID card said, "The Aristide Foundation," and no one else on the staff seemed to have this sort of contact. For good or ill, the idea was to keep communication channels open.

Markington was always nervous, and seemed to fear that his transfer of information to me might have dire consequences. Or it could have been an act. Not knowing their provenance or accuracy, I really had no interest in the contents of his lists. But my staunch and stated policy in the office was, "Any lunatic gets a moment with me." And I admit I was curious what was behind them, and why he came to me.

I took his hit lists in early May, then filed them away and forgot I even had them, until July, 2012, when I thought it would be time to write this up.

I didn't know Markington had been picked up temporarily in May 2000 as a suspect in the Dominique killing. Whether he was set up as "bait" to get the U.S. Embassy or me implicated, I never figured out. He was not "arrested" or "detained" or "indicted," but in the lacking vocabulary of Haitian justice, was accompanied by someone, involuntarily, somewhere.

June 24, a Saturday, my home phone woke me up at 7:00 am or so. At the other end was WL, a Haitian official I'd met a year earlier. Now he was "unofficially" investigating the Dominique murder.

He said, "I have your friend here, Philippe Markington." He handed the phone to Markington and I recognized the voice.

Markington said, "Why haven't you given [WL] the $2,000 he asked for?" He said he would send WL Monday to my office to pick up the money.

I imagined Markington in some dark dungeon with a gun to his head, which turned out to be exactly the case. I told Markington to drop the whole idea and not to send WL to see me. I said that if he had anything to tell me, he should come to my office Monday to do so. "But where are you?" I asked again, and there was no answer. WL took the phone back.

"Your friend Markington is in a bit of trouble," WL said. "It will cost you some money to get him out."

Was Markington their former collaborator, now dumped like sheep to feed the piranhas? Or had he never been taken by them in the first place? Or was it an elaborate *trompe l'oeil* for some occult purpose?

I wrote memos the next few days to keep track of the chain of events.

June 26, the sort-of prosecutor in the case called me at home and asked to come over. I said no, but I would meet him the bar of the Hotel Montana (since rebuilt after being destroyed in the 2010 earthquake).

WL, quite agitated, was not his previous, friendly self. He said he'd seen Markington earlier the same day, and asked again for $2,000 for Markington's release. He insinuated I must have some "debts" to Markington, and likely needed him for purposes of information.

The rest of the conversation went like this:

Him: "What did Markington give you that created a debt on your behalf?"
Me: "Absolutely nothing."
Him: "I wouldn't have wasted my time on a Friday night if I had known you don't have $2,000 to hand over to me."
Me: "You asked for the meeting. I didn't."
Him: "You are not a real friend to Markington."
Me: "I never said I was."

The prosecutor became very aggressive, and my patience ran thin. Disdainfully I took out six *gourdes* from my pocket (about 45 cents U.S.), threw them on the table, and left. Weeks later, the act was cited as an insulting "down payment" on the $2,000. The prosecutor stopped me on my way out. "Careful, this could be threatening to you."

Me: "Threats of what, injury? Death, expulsion?"
Him: "You diplomats all think you have special privileges."
Me: "Unfair, perhaps, but true. I know only that one day I will leave Haiti. Whether it is sooner or later is not a major factor to me."
Him: "You think you can make it to the airport any time, but even as you walk across the tarmac, you're not safe until you're in the airplane."

Friends more versed in the language of Haiti than I was later told me this was a death threat.

The prosecutor remained his tawdry self until the end, asking agitatedly if he himself was on one of Markington's hit lists. In an act of striking bravado, he asked me for a U.S. government-sponsored trip to the United States.

I understood then that all that was wrong with Haiti was derived from fear, the one Haitian afraid of the other. It doesn't take a genius to know this about the country, but that day I got it through the pores of my skin.

A snarky embassy colleague said to me (not exactly accurately), "Whitman, you got yourself into this, now let's see you get yourself out."

"Interrogatoire" (Part Three)

August 5, 2012

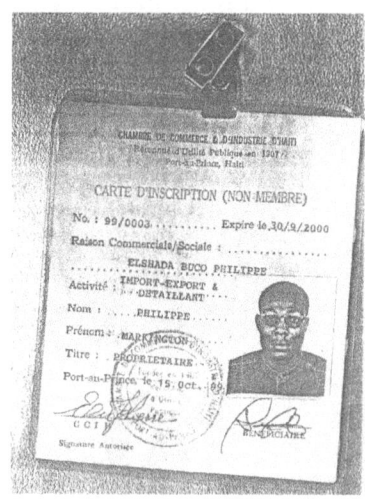

[Part three of four] In a May 30 statement to the local daily *Le Nouvelliste*, assassination suspect and Haitian senator Dany Toussaint mentioned my name and said, "Why does an embassy spokesman need permission to maintain contact with a hired killer? Never mind. I'll say more when the time is right." Two years before his death, Dominique had named Toussaint as his likely assassin. This was beginning to be creepy.

The Haitian police cooked up an internal memo (leaked to the press, and from the press to me), noting that a white Jeep Cherokee had been spotted at the scene of the crime April 3, and that I owned a vehicle of that description. There were tens of thousands of others on the island, by the way. No mention of any license number.

True enough: the intrepid Jeep followed me to three continents. I had a certain affection for it, though it kept breaking down on treacherous country roads. The police memo didn't have many spellings correct, but cited a Markington ("Mackington")-Whitman ("Wittman") connection. President Préval, Justice Minister Camille LeBlanc, and Police Chief Paul Denizé were all copied on the memo. WL, the sort-of prosecutor, was mentioned in the police memo simply as "The Coordinator."

August 10, Justice Minister LeBlanc called the embassy and asked them to send me in for a chat. Something about the impugned honor of "The Coordinator" in the case.

A helpful colleague said, "They're not supposed to do that sort of thing except in a diplomatic note through the foreign ministry. But you'll need a witness, so let's go and get it over with." We made an appointment for 9:30am, August 11. I had never been convoked by a minister in any country and couldn't remember ever having sat down with one.

My colleague Rick (not his real name) and I got to the justice ministry that day; the building defied description but I'll try:

A rickety mass ready to crumble on itself, the early nineteenth-century building had ghostly remnants of an ornate, earlier age. Fallen into complete neglect and disrepair, the walls and floors creaked; I think a layer of mold lay over the ancient paint and varnish, now peeled and rotting.

Rick and I were directed down the building's longest hallway, where armed men stood in and out of uniform every two meters or so, slouched, heavily armed, each in different garb and with different weapons. Most seemed exhausted. They noticed but did not acknowledge us. An adjutant left us in the waiting area by the minister's office.

As we waited, Rick said to me in an inspired moment, "Make sure you give the minister your business card on the way in."

I winked back and was grateful for an insight which could later save the day, if it was well played.

The minister received us pretty cordially. There were no armed guards in the inner office, but when we entered we saw The Coordinator already stationed there, scowling at us and especially at me. I gave the minister my card.

The ministerial style was in place, with some greetings and friendly comments. After some preliminaries, the minister gestured to the scowling prosecutor, and said to me, "My colleague says you claim he tried to get $2,000 out of you over the Markington affair."

I said, "Well, he did."

I expected the worst, but to my surprise, the prosecutor ("coordinator") corroborated this himself, and explained to his boss that the point was to see if there was a U.S. Embassy link to the murder. There wasn't much to say on anybody's part in response.

The minister acknowledged (for the first time officially) that Haitian authorities had Markington in custody. He paused for me to react, but again, there was nothing much to say. The room was tense.

"Mr. Whitman, when Markington was detained, he claimed he was a good friend of yours, and pulled your business card out of his wallet to prove it."

I glanced at Rick for cues, then decided the time had come to wing it. I said to the minister, "Lots of people in this town have my business card. I believe *you* have one also. May I ask, does that mean you killed Jean Dominique?"

Rick was silently delighted, the minister laughed, and even the prosecutor loosened up a little. Clearly there wasn't much here to investigate.

The minister had coffee brought in, and everything was amiable from then on. If his goal was to get me and the prosecutor to shake hands and settle our differences, I guess he succeeded.

Rick and I were relieved, and stepped back out into the normal, tropical air outside, from the stale and oppressive stench of those confined hallways. We still wondered what the hell this whole thing was about.

But Where is Markington? (Part Four)

August 6, 2012

[Part four of four] The question was, and still is, whatever happened to Markington? Was he in some dungeon in chains, or dead, or clandestinely running the country? Had he indeed been at the scene of the crime April 3, or even one of a passel of hitmen? And for what purpose? Paid by Dany Toussaint, or by the regime itself? A chit for the faltering government?

One afternoon in September 2000, there was a stir in the outer reception of my public affairs office. In the old days, we were on the third floor of a commercial building, 100 yards from the embassy. A lot had happened along those 100 yards over the years, and my protective employees did everything to keep me from walking the short distance twice a day to attend meetings at the chancery. The Rond-Point Harry Truman gave us a view of one of the most gruesome urban areas in the world. Gang warfare, marching mobs, and suffocating crowds populated the roundabout. We witnessed the murder of a suspected thief, killed by the market workers for lifting an avocado. We had gotten used to it.

I stepped out to see what the commotion was about in the outer office. The employees looked very afraid. They'd seen most everything and knew better than I when something was really off.

"Monsieur Whitman, the building is surrounded by armed men. They are heading upstairs."

I didn't want any massacres on my watch.

Our embassy-employed guard downstairs was a real gentleman, and not of much use in a situation like this. He wasn't even allowed to have weapons, so there wasn't much protection.

We heard the sound of boots and metal coming up the steps to the third floor. Some of my employees hid under their desks. I'd never seen them so scared.

The office door opened from the hallway, and some mean-looking hombres stepped in. What had seemed to be a platoon of gangsters was in fact a group of four armed men (two in police uniform, two not). They had a lot of rounds of ammunition, and there didn't seem much point in making a fuss. I asked them what they wanted.

They didn't say much, but brought in a prisoner from the hallway. The prisoner was handcuffed and had the vacant look of a desperado. He was gaunt, slow to move, and had burns on his arms.

I didn't recognize him right away, but it was Markington.

He wasn't the robust and swaggering young man I'd known months before, and he seemed about 50 pounds thinner.

"What's going on?" I asked the armed foursome.

One of the officers pulled out a piece of paper. "The engineer Philippe Markington has permission to spend one hour in the city under armed escort," he said. "He asked to be brought to see you."

I said, "Permission from where? Is he in detention, and are you police?" But there were no answers. Fear deepened among the staff.

Markington didn't look well, not at all. Actually he looked like a dying man. Everyone in the room was nervous, the policemen no less than the rest of us. They had all the power but didn't seem to know what to do with it, nor what was supposed to come next.

"The prisoner has asked for ten minutes alone with you in your office," one said.

I didn't know what to make of it, but had to think of something to do.

"You tell me what you want," I said to the armed men, whose weapons seemed to mean business.

One of the police shrugged and said, "As you wish." I made him repeat it.

Probably stupidly (but swayed by curiosity), I said, "He can come into my office, but only if you point those things away from my workers."

The one in charge removed Markington's handcuffs and ordered the others to lower their weapons.

With some dread, I took the ghostly Markington, alone, into my office. I still thought this could be some horrendous trick, but I couldn't think of any better options at that moment.

Markington took a seat on my couch and had some trouble sitting up. I asked him what the hell was going on.

"Monsieur Whitman, they torture me every day to get me to denounce you, but I won't."

"Philippe, many thanks, but denounce me for what? And who are these people and where do they keep you?"

"I don't even know. But they want me to say you are a spy and I'm your agent. I won't do it, because you're not, and I'm not."

"This is very honorable, Philippe," I said. 'But please tell them anything you need to in order to stop being tortured. Is there something I can do for you?"

"Nothing can be done for me," he said morosely. "And I won't denounce you if I have to tell a lie to do so."

I was moved and puzzled, in equal amounts.

"This is nuts," I said to the pitifully reduced being half lying on the couch. "Do they burn you?" I said, pointing at his arms.

"Cigarettes, other things."

I had never liked Markington, but always saw him as an enigma—now even more so. It seemed the least likely hypothesis, but maybe he had been telling the truth all along.

The armed men came in the room, said time was up, and took him away. I never saw him or them again.

That is exactly what happened. Expect no answers, because there were none. I was as attached and detached from Markington as I would be from any man in a dreadful predicament. I knew there was no help for him. I owed my workers my best attention to try to calm them down.

I still don't know who the engineer Philippe Markington really was or what he was about, or what became of him, or whether he is alive or dead today. I return to the original question:

Where is Philippe Markington?

They used to say of Haiti (but it applies to many places), "Believe nothing of what you hear in this place. And only half of what you see."

Reading from Africa

August 10, 2012

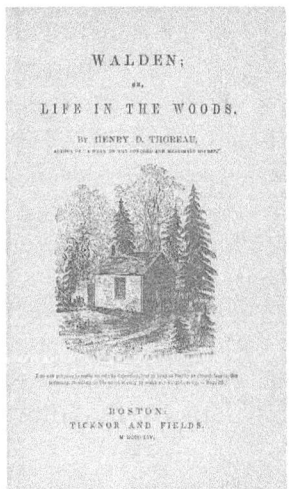

This is a story mainly of grateful memories. Long stays in Africa—especially the evenings after early dusk—call for reading in the old fashion, where like wine tasters, the reader savors, spits, savors again, then considers the pleasure somehow a form of achievement.

For the overbunked American (distractions, gadgets, famished addicts sucking at the teats of mass communication), a night in Africa with the television and Internet down can be a blessing. This would be reading as it must have been for early discoverers of Twain, Dreiser, James, Wharton.

The non-profit Library of America puts out volumes of America's classics, now often overlooked in the din of contemporary clatter. U.S. Embassies collect these in their information resource centers (IRCs). We used to call them "libraries," but retrenchment politics of the 1990s forbade the use of the word. The series sit like remote monuments in the stacks of American IRCs in nearly every country.

If you just pick one up, you'll find the never-bent spines of these books grateful for your attention. Give them your first fifteen minutes, and they take over like transporting seraphim.

My first adventure of this sort was Thoreau, which I reread in Brazzaville in 1980. I mean *Walden*, of course. I'd "read" it in high school seventeen years earlier, but in the drifting nights of Central Africa, to the song of the bullfrog in mating season, I took just one chapter per evening, and I think absorbed Thoreau's tone and intentions, maybe almost as slowly as he wrote it. This was not a task, but a gain at no cost. The harried Westerner can benefit from time passing where the present has no set value, but is all and everywhere. This is the way humanity has lived in most places at most times.

Other readings happened, mainly in places where neighbors expected little of their days and nights. The gas lamp—still the vehicle of evening vision in third world countries—is relegated to the museum and to movie depictions for the impoverished modern man and woman.

In Yaoundé, Cameroon, I cheated and experienced Proust. "Cheated" by reading a non-American, and by going with a fine English translation when I'd reached 60 and realized I "should" but never would read him in his original French. I also broke open the weighty tomes (I owned these ones) and took small scissored sections to bed, where I went through the entire work, remembering some passages better than others.

They say Proust is as much a meditation as a cognitive experience. It may be so. I remember the immense weight at the ends of his long sentences, especially toward the dénouement of Remembrance, where he names many of his fictional and semi-fictional characters fallen in the trenches of World War I. "So-and-so, so-and-so, and furthermore ...all ...dead." Unforgettable the impact, even if the names slip away.

For this type of pastime, it's probably better to have only a few contacts and little knowledge of the exotic place where you are. Two summers ago in Conakry, Guinea, I took out some of the less well-known essays of Mark Twain from the IRC, and the memoirs of his friend Ulysses S. Grant. I'm sure no one had cracked open the latter, and that few in today's world have plowed through the Grant's entire story (who has time?). His bewildered recollections of the Mexican War showed him to be a humanist and humorist. When he laments the pitiful state of Mexican soldiers in that senseless war, he shows pity for them even as he cuts them down.

At the end of his Civil War reflections—by which time he was in acute suffering from advanced throat cancer—he said, remarkably, "I never doubted the sincerity of my enemies." This sentiment towers even over magnanimity. Grant's prose is among the most noble ever written by a warrior.

I also found Brian Urquhart's biography of Ralph Bunche that summer, and understood for the first time the phrase, "We call on all parties..." These foolish, empty words are uttered by most governments every day like a moron's catechism. They once had meaning because Ralph Bunche stood behind them, so people listened, even in the Middle East. Now, in Bunche's absence, the phrase usually rings hollow.

I came upon Michael Beschloss's and Strobe Talbott's amazingly-detailed *At the Highest Levels: The Inside Story of the End of the Cold War*. I think I understand now how it happened between Bush and Gorbachev.

For Accra, Ghana, in 2011, there were Saul Bellow's letters, and the now suddenly-relevant Nicholas Shaxson's *Treasure Islands*, about offshore bank accounts.

Further down the road, these weeks in Lagos, I've picked up James Thurber, everyone's forgotten favorite sage, whose essays were "selected" for the Library of America edition by Garrison Keillor, who of course put "Is Sex Necessary?" at the head of the list. Who knew that America's finest essay on the city of Paris came from the Midwestern humorist (I mean, the earlier one)? Thurber was there in 1918 when the city was waking from the same war depicted in late Proust: "Her heart was warm and gay, all right, but there was hysteria in its beat, and the kind of compulsive elation psychiatrists strive to cure."

I think Thurber rises above his famous contemporaries in remembering post-World War I Paris: "I have had my moments of depression and worry about the great city, but I have never felt that I was sitting up at night with a fatally sick friend."

Thurber joins but transcends others who have cited Paris not to project an image of their own sophistication, but to mark humble wonder. He reminds us that Paris has risen out of "war, ultimatum, occupation, domestic upheaval, cabinet crises, international tension, and dark prophecy, as it has been in the habit of doing since its residents saw the menacing glitter of Roman shields many centuries ago."

This passage would have been unknown to me if the General Services Officer in Lagos had ever managed to get my television cable working in August of 2012. Most grateful.

Likewise, the potent diatribe against lingering McCarthyism, in Thurber's 1956 allegory "The Peacelike Mongoose," where the non-cobra-baiting eccentric mongoose is accused of being "mongoosexual" by his peers and detractors: "Ashes to ashes, clay to clay, if the enemy doesn't get you your own folks may." Thurber and Walt Kelly were a good team on this.

In an essay from 1937, Thurber talks of "the kind of night in which the wind moans in the wires, and telephone bells ringing without benefit of human agency, and there are inexplicable sounds of doors and windows." These times almost don't exist anymore in a world of working power grids.

Rewards of reading unhampered by distraction can be unsought, undeserved, but I recommend them to anyone who wants a truly cheap thrill. Turn off everything else if possible, and take the classics. They haven't been replaced. And don't be put off by a rack of tomes in black binding with the names of some you avoided—or had to take like castor oil—in high school.

Turf Issues

August 14, 2012

Ronnie the Rat scowled at me from the opposite end of the largest living room I've ever been in. He was like a science fiction mutation, about the size of a nearly full-grown pony. Well, about a foot long, plus another foot for his tail and you get two feet from head to tail tip. I mean, really.

Granted, the house and its living room were not "mine," but belonged to the U.S. Embassy in Yaoundé, which had me live in for my tour in Cameroon. But I worked, and the house was part of what I got in return.

"I work too, bottom-feeder," the rat seemed to say. He hyperventilated, I think more from disgust than fight-or-flight. He was surveying the situation and making strategy.

Usually I have an affinity for mammals, and I know every rat has a mother. Still, I don't like bullies, and I wanted my living space to myself. We stared at each other from about three meters apart. In the Völsunga saga, we would have been exchanging insults from opposite sides of narrow bodies of water.

Mammals' strategies in disputes (even lizards') are not all that different from one another: avoid actual conflict if you can while retaining an advantage; retreat when necessary; attack only when you have overwhelming strength (the Powell Doctrine); and above all, see if intimidation can work. Maintain communication even if you intend not to negotiate. ICBMs and phased-array radars are fancy devices, but fall exactly into these categories.

Ronnie and I established our red lines. In my best rat-ese I said, "It's true I don't need all this space. But let's be clear: you stay in the kitchen, where everything edible is locked up in the refrigerator anyway. The rest of the house is for me."

Ronnie responded, more to the point, "My arse."

He had an attitude. I understood he desired life and shelter, and had some claim to them. But he was two feet long, really ugly, and maybe carried rabies. He sent rejection signals to all my proposed arrangements. His nasty whiskers twitched and his repugnant little hyperventilating abdomen conveyed rat swear words (must be worse than ours) and hatred for me.

"Who do you suppose built this thing?" he communicated to me.

"Actually, my people did," I said. "Not yours."

"My arse," he said. "It was here long before you got here, and me too. It's mine as much as yours."

I wasn't in a mood for palaver. I stomped on the floor (no reaction at all from him) and went to the back bedroom and to hell with it.

Ronnie was a provocateur, and came the next evening to stake out his space again in the living room, albeit from the far end. I tried another dialect of rat-ese, and said, "One more time. You in the kitchen where there is nothing for you anyway, me in the rest of the house. Capisc'?" Ronnie again glared at me with ratacious indignation.

Rats are smart, and know how to navigate the crannies of other species' dwellings. They find holes we can't see, and know how to shut up and disappear even an hour before a human clomps into the house. I think they know that running between our legs, aside from being great sport, disgusts and terrifies us. Maybe they know that we know that they might carry rabies and they taunt us: "Tetanus! Lockjaw! Human scum!" Like us, they use what they have for strategic advantage.

I went to the embassy and asked the housing office for help.

"We don't do rats," they said.

"Don't do rats? What do you do?" I asked.

"We don't do traps, and we don't do poison. It's a liability thing; children could be hurt."

"The nearest child is a kilometer away," I said.

"It's policy," they answered.

I made a last effort at conciliation with Ronnie, but he would have none of it. To him, I was the intruder. He was awfully large, even if I was larger. He was a lot quicker and more nimble than I was, and (did I mention?) maybe he carried rabies.

I got a trap and cheese from the local market and left it by the stove.

"Surely you jest," the message seemed to say the following morning, the trap still set and the cheese neatly gone.

Then I got a cardboard plate with very strong glue at the edges, so the bait in the middle got the adversary totally stuck without pain or amputation.

"Dimwit!" was the message the next morning, the bait completely removed.

I didn't like Ronnie's tone. I went back to the market and found a plastic bag that said, "This substance is so poisonous you must not even touch the bag or perforate it in any way. Just place it, untouched, in the area where it is needed. Go nowhere near it for 24 hours."

I didn't want to escalate to the Doomsday Weapon, but the embassy and Ronnie left me no choice. I carried the sack of poison inside another sack, then inside another, and left it in the usual place by the stove. I guess Agent Orange would be like herbal aroma therapy compared to this stuff.

Sure enough, the next day the sack was pierced, Ronnie had left his Zorro mark. No sign of Ronnie, though, and there hadn't been any bait this time, so I guess he fell for it. Must have had Scent of Rosalind Rat. To get the adversary, if all else fails, appeal below the belt.

A couple of days later I saw Ronnie, defenses down, doing a sort of foxtrot in the pantry. He never mentioned if he was in euphoria or agony, just went trance-like through the neutral zone between kitchen and living room. I felt a little sorry since his future did not look bright.

I took a plastic bucket and threw it over him.

Then I thought, "Einstein! What do I do now with a live rat under a bucket?" I asked the day guard at the gate to remove Ronnie, no questions asked.

It turns out that rat is a delicacy in Cameroon, and the guard seized the opportunity. I cautioned him about the poison, but he did whatever he did, and Ronnie was gone. The guard was thrilled.

I won't say I missed Ronnie, but neither did I miss Joe, the human roommate I'd had in Brookline, Massachusetts, in 1968-69. Ronald R. Rat, circa 2005-2005. He was born, he lived, he finished. I don't know much about his quality of life, but his wishes were clear, and his defiance lasted until the very end.

An Overnight in Mainz

September 30, 2012

If you're reading this, chances are you have either had a layover in Frankfurt's airport at some point or have tried to avoid doing so. Morning arrival, four hours to departure, and what to do: get euros (or not) and shop your way through FRA's dozens of sleek boutiques? They are basically ATL or DFW with umlauts.

Other options include stretching out over three waiting-room seats and striking the corpse pose, hoping friends or colleagues will not notice you at it, or getting an overpriced room at one of the airport hotels or way stations. Carve out 24 hours from your low-tolerance schedule, though, and there is a far better option.

I asked Asunción, my consultant on these matters, how to break up a recent trip from Lagos (don't ask) to Washington, connecting through Frankfurt.

"Time to see Heidelberg, I guess," I said. "I can spend the extra day and I guess I'll be fried from the overnight from Lagos."

"Too far from the airport," Asunción said. "Why not just go to Mainz?"

"Mainz, what is that?" I asked.

"How should I know?" Asunción answered. "I've never been there."

Asunción's intuitions are never wrong, so I booked a hotel 55 yards (meters are about the same) from the Mainz train station. The Internet said the train went straight from the Frankfurt airport to Mainz's Hauptbahnhof in half an hour. It didn't seem likely, but I went for it.

I knew I'd want a nap and shower the morning I got there, so I booked the room for the previous night to make sure. Two nights at the perfectly convenient and clean Schottenhof Hotel came out much cheaper than a single night—2:00pm check-in—would have been at any of the fancy Frankfurt airport hotels.

Mainz is the perfect town for a relaxed overnight. The super-quick S-Bahn from the airport to Mainz (4 euro 20, or six dollars) took thirteen minutes door-to-door. Taking the puddle jumper back the next day (if you consider the majestic Rhine River a puddle) lagged in at 27 minutes, same price.

The shady, short street facing the Hauptbahnhof has two or three 70-dollar hotels, and one 3-star, with four sidewalk cafés and no artificial sources of noise.

I arrived on the day of a heat wave (mid-eighties! *Ach, du lieber!*), and I have empirical evidence that rain and clouds never threaten the skies above this charming town, or at least they didn't on August 18-19 of 2012.

I think Germans are mostly in Mallorca or Ibiza during the third week of August. Anyway, the town was delightfully not crowded.

I had my nap and shower in room 207 of the Schottenhof, then went out with my city map to see this delightful town. A two-car choo-choo train on rubber wheels rolled past as I walked down the Kaiserstrasse—a smaller version of Boston's Commonweatlth Avenue—under shade on a sunny day. I avoided the glance of the driver because I don't do choo-choo trains with commentary. But I admit I followed the vehicle, walking toward the Rhein and stopping in the Christus Kirche to see what Protestantism was like in central Germany in the early twentieth century. The Catholic cathedral is a 10- or 15-minute walk toward the *altstadt* (old city); in fact you can circumnavigate the city on foot in 30 minutes. But why would you, with so many bistros and coffee houses along the way?

I crossed the Grosse Bleiche with my map, and a friendly Mainzer asked if I needed help.

"Not really," I said. "But if you had time to see just one museum, which on would it be?"

"The Landesmuseum, just there," she said in perfect English. "It's not on your map, but you'll like it."

I walked in that direction, but never made it. A coffee house too charming to pass up got in the way, around Bahnhofstrasse. I stopped in for a cold couscous salad and a "macchiato," which in Germany is more like a steamed milk and a dash of expresso. It comes with a tasty biscuit the size of a dime, and is just enough for restoration on a walking tour.

My lunch cost eight euro 50 (about $11), and was just about perfect.

The Landesmuseum was just across a tranquil intersection. It was only 2:00pm and I'd seen half the city. I settled in with my Kindle for a few minutes. When I looked up I saw Antonia K at the next table, one of my favorite students from the previous spring term in Washington. I saw her first, and thought jet lag might be playing tricks.

"Professor Whitman! In Mainz! What are the chances?" Antonia said to her friend Marie, a college student about to be a school teacher. Like Antonia, Marie's English was perfect. But she would be teaching Spanish once the exams freed her to do so.

I said, "I thought you were from Frankfurt!"

"I say that because in the U.S. people don't know where Mainz is," Antonia said.

She took me through the *altstadt*, which includes the little house where one Johannes Gutenberg did something with moveable type in 1450.

"We can stop for a drink," she said, midway through the *altstadt*.

"I don't suppose there might be some beer somewhere in Mainz?" I asked.

"It's possible," Antonia said.

"Maybe imported from Belgium?" I teased.

"Maybe," she said.

She had a late afternoon appointment to rescue a troubled love affair between two friends. I released her for this noble endeavor, and walked the ten minutes back to the Schottenhof for a second nap.

Then I strolled through Mainz's tranquil August streets at early dinner time, the glow of the evening sky meeting the candles on the bistro tables everywhere. I passed up a dozen alluring sidewalk eateries only because each one seemed to lead to the next. I settled in one called the Pascha, a Turkish family restaurant. When it was time to order, I said, "*Ich kann nicht so gut Deutsch sprache.*"

"Me neither," said the tavern owner. I got something called a Turkish pizza—delicious and three times more than I could eat, for four euro—plus mineral water and spicy *aubergine forshpeise*—for a total bill of eight euro 60. I realized that even in small Mainz, I should have taken Antonia's number so I could invite her to breakfast the next day. The kindly hotel manager at the Schottenhof called the local information number on his cell phone and handed it to me. "*Frau oder Fraulein?*" the operator asked when I gave Antonia's name and street address.

"*Fraulein,*" I said.

"Sorry, then I can't give you the number," the operator said protectively.

"*Macht nichts,*" I said, using up most of the rest of my German vocabulary.

I slept soundly, woke up fine, and had the hotel breakfast (included). I walked the 55 yards back to the train station, and got my 4 euro 40 S-Bahn ticket back to the Frankfurt airport.

Just to make sure, after getting on the train from Platform 4A, I asked a passenger, "*Ist das den S-Bahn nach Frankfurt Lufthaven?*" I was pretty proud of my efforts.

The passenger said, "You mean the airport? Yes, this is the one."

The second stop on the puddle jumper is 30 feet from the "Romische Teater," the remains of a Roman theater from 80 B.C. Six stops later, I was back at Terminal One of the airport, well ahead of schedule for my flight back to Washington IAD.

The Dog is Well

December 30, 2012

I haven't heard Sonja Vesterholt's actual voice in some years, but it came back with immediacy when I read her prose on a flight from Copenhagen to Baltimore last week. Learning more about your friends is both unsettling and satisfying. In the 1980s in Denmark, I'd heard some of her stories from the earlier days in the Soviet Union. Now came the book, *Hunden er rask* ("The dog is well"), Gyldendal, 2011.

In 1970, Sonja ("Sonia" in English) immigrated to Denmark after marrying Ole Vesterholt, a Danish student of Slavic languages. Ole was already deceased when I met Sonja in 1987, as were her first husband Osha, her first child Alyosha, her father, and her mother. Nazis killed 27 million shortly before her birth in 1945. If that weren't enough, before and after the war, Stalin turned against his own people, killing tens of millions more in the gulags. Only handfuls of errant Marxists in the West believed any of communism's pretenses during the Stalin and Krushchev eras, when Soviet citizens saw pretty clearly through their system despite its watertight controls on information.

Sonja's mother had survived the 900-day Nazi siege of Leningrad in World War II, thanks partly to a cat-turned-meal in the winter of 1942. Two million died in that still-gorgeous city, now Saint Petersburg.

After Sonja's immigration to Denmark and Ole's death, she moved to an apartment with the lofty ceilings, cavernous spaces, broad sweeps of ensuite rooms, and the west-facing picture windows one thinks of in an idealized Saint Petersburg parlor from the time of Pushkin or Goncharov. She never lived that way herself in her first 25 years; rather, in a 12-meter-square flat with a communal kitchen stove backed up to the upright piano she worked on, as adjunct to a dance instructor in the 1960s to make ends meet.

Hunden er rask is a vivid account of a life in an immense country based on false premises. As her invalid mother's sole caregiver, Sonja was excused from public school and Komsomol camp as a child—whence, perhaps, the origin of her independent thinking. Defiance became her main feature.

The book's title comes from a telegram received by Sonja'a mother one day in 1952, after a dog bite resulted in 40 painful anti-rabies shots to Sonja's stomach. Soviet authorities, snooping on every aspect of everyone's lives, took the short message to be a coded action of espionage or insurrection, until Sonja's mother was able to demonstrate its real meaning at the local post office: she had her daughter lift her skirt to show the needle marks on her abdomen. Escaping imprisonment, torture, or execution, the mother and daughter were free to go after showing that the message had to do with the dog bite during a summer vacation on the Baltic, where Sonja had been born. "The dog is well"—no rabies. Soviet authorities were crude, stupid, sycophantic, mendacious, and mostly sadistic, but they differed from Nazis in their inconsistency, and the occasional act of mercy and even generosity.

The enemy was the system, not individuals. Sonja's father, a 50-year member of the Communist Party, came clean to an estranged daughter only at the end of his life—and even then, in coded, epistolary language. Sonja had said, "Fuck your mother" to KGB interrogators when they tried to recruit her on the eve of her departure with her new Danish husband. She was punished years later for this, refused a visa back to the USSR to attend her father's funeral.

One cannot call "lachrymose" a clear and dry account of tragedy. This simple narrative merely tells what happened, from birth in 1945 to emigration in 1970 and beyond. Sonja's saga is that of a survivor, with extreme privation, a KGB car in front of her house for the six months of her illegal cohabitation with her Danish future husband. Millions of others suffered the same fate or worse, but few records this good exist, of how it was from day to day.

Hunden er rask draws the reader into the joys of motherhood during Alyosha's birth in 1966 and the sorrow of his death later the same year. Sonja says, with stark candor, "We were so young, and our marriage could not survive the loss of a child."

The account traces the jubilation of the Soviet people on the day of Yuri Gargarin's Sputnik triumph of 1961, after the first orbited spacecraft in 1956. Because science fiction was the favorite genre of a nation forbidden to discuss its real situation, the Sputnik triumph triggered spontaneous joy on April 12, 1961. Vesterholt describes the demonstrations as the first non-contrived ones in the country's history, idiotically broken up by a befuddled Soviet police at Red Square the same day.

Sonja was always a phenom in Copenhagen. All who knew her or fell in her wide circle of friends and colleagues revered her. Garrison Keillor was fascinated by her, and had her to a communal celebration with his Danish wife in the spring of 1988. In her book, Sonja goes easy on her reception by Danes in 1970. In her interview with editor Herbert Pundik included in the book's afterword, she cites the Vesterholt family's warm welcome for their new daughter-in-law.

In fact, Danish xenophobia was a strong force during her period as immigrant. I saw it clearly at the time. "Generosity," would say those who have known Sonja. But defiance and a harsh light on hypocrisy, foolishness, with disdain for "talentless would-be professionals"—these strong traits marked her as well.

The latter chapters in the book are simply heart-breaking, but bear not a hint of preening or exhibitionism. "A Happy Death" describes the Sonja's mother's last day in 1975. Paralyzed by a stroke years before, she got a washcloth bath administered by her visiting daughter. The mother had time to say, "I am so happy." Then she died, "within a second."

The chapter entitled "My father" cites letters written by an estranged father seeking reconciliation at the end of his life in 1983. The chapter includes the text of Sonja's impassioned request to Soviet authorities asking permission to visit. Though a similar one had worked in 1975 for her to visit her failing mother, the 1983 one was denied.

This locally-popular memoir will be scripted for stage presentation in fall of 2013 in Copenhagen. The book is dedicated "to Anna," Sonja's remarkable daughter, now a mother to her own two-year-old. Sometimes the greatest accomplishments are the unplanned ones. Sonja's lifelong duel with the Soviet system yielded a daughter and granddaughter, both strong-willed and making their own marks. *Hunden er rask* is not available yet in other languages. But it ought to be, for the sake of living history, and a view of the occasional triumph of humanity over ideology.

Vladimir

December 31, 2012

Vladimir Pimonov stepped out of the USSR first in 1988. The Soviet authorities didn't want to allow him to leave and kept him under house arrest in 1987, but they were getting a beating in the Danish press for being, well, Soviet-like, and now we know the system was close to collapse. So they threw in the towel and gave him the exit visa.

Volodya arrived at the Copenhagen train station later that year, greeted by hundreds of émigrés and journalists. He was very famous for about two weeks, then slipped into obscurity. Back in the USSR, Volodya had done his academic work on Shakespeare—*Hamlet* in particular—and published many articles on Russia's national sport, chess. He appears in the 1988 book *Searching for Bobby Fischer* by Fred Waitzkin. We forget that chess was the precursor to video games and war simulations from an earlier age and was an enactment of all-out war for centuries, though with freeze-frames between the moves.

He said, "To understand Russia, it's not enough to know Kremlinology; you must know chess and ballet as well."

I put him in touch with Sven Ove Gade, editor at that time for the Danish tabloid *Ekstra Bladet*. At the U.S. Embassy, we used to parse the daily take from the more "serious" dailies (*Politiken, Berlingske Tidende, Information*...) but mostly ignored the tabloids, which had over twice the circulation of the serious ones combined. There seemed an inexhaustible supply of Danish teenage girls (and a few 40-year-olds) ready to decorate the tabloid's page nine al fresco, and this no doubt kept the circulation at reliable levels. Gade, however, was determined to make the paper into a premier exposé vanguard as well, and to add serious investigative pieces to its mix. Over the next twenty years, he managed to do so.

He "interviewed" Volodya for a job in late 1988, and asked a single question: "So what do you think you can do for me?"

Volodya answered, "How can you ask such a question? Isn't it obvious? I'm Russian."

Gade hired him on the spot. Volodya kept the job for 23 years.

Volodya had sources in Moscow, wide and deep. They all sang to him over the phone. He broke late Cold War stories, and scooped Europe's more famous dailies in UK, Germany, France, and elsewhere.

With Gade's full trust and backing, and almost no editorial interference, Volodya published pieces exposing prominent Danes benefiting from KGB financial backing, and a scoop on Yeltsin's health problems, drawing rebukes from Germany Chancellor Helmuth Kohl. But the scoop was right.

Pimonov's stories ran much counter to Danish paradigms, and Danes didn't appreciate it. I don't think Volodya had a vendetta against the Soviet Union or anyone else in particular, but his stories were red flags (pardon the expression) and did no more than assist a corrupt Moscow regime in indicting itself in Western eyes. The stories drifted to other dailies in Europe, and in their modest way probably accelerated the rapid removal of the veil over Soviet hollowness.

More painfully, Volodya's *Ekstra Bladet* outed Danish collaborators and others on the take of the KGB's modest handouts. A local journalist obsessed over the possible irregularities of the NATO radar in Thule in northern Greenland, and even developed a logo for his daily diatribes. He argued the Thule base was a violation of the 1972 ABM treaty, even as NATO said the same of Krasnoyarsk in Russia.

With colleague Jakob Andersen, Volodya also tracked down evidence the KGB was financing similar articles and showing its appreciation monetarily to the Danish journalist.

Forgiveness for one more pun, but this crossed a red line in Danish society. Tacit codes of conduct required the "cold shoulder" at worst for social misdemeanors and outings of individuals by foreigners, but never explicit naming and shaming. The libel case then initiated by the Thule journalist is only now in the Danish Supreme Court for adjudication, 25 years later.

Volodya also traced the KBG's material support for Yasser Arafat's terrorist activities prior to his winning the Nobel Peace Prize in 1994, and Moscow's (illegal) financial favors for Danish communist leader Ole Sohn.

In 2006, working with colleagues Bo Elkjaer and John Mynderup, Volodya published a series of articles on the alleged money laundering for Russian oligarchs by banks in Iceland, accurately predicting the 2008 demise of one of them, Kaupthing.

Volodya was shunned, and his own colleagues at *Ekstra Bladet* found him indigestible foreign matter. People said he had a lack of social lubricant; I call it journalistic integrity. He was hurt by his isolation, but he never pandered for popularity.

Volodya's passion for Shakespeare surpassed his temporal achievements. His work on "minimal plot" found expression in his doctoral thesis, "The Poetics of Theatricality in Shakespeare's Drama," published in 2004.

Twenty years after I met him, I was driving down the street in Cameroon's capital, Yaoundé, and saw a commercial banner stretching out over the road, offering "specials" on Swiss Air flights to Moscow. These banners usually offered deals on underwear in bulk, or newly imported cell phones or cognac. The ad seemed directed to a very tiny target group, possibly only me.

I went for the bait and booked a ticket for Moscow, where I'd never been. I contacted Volodya who was back in Moscow after the Iron Curtain had fallen. At that time he was *Ekstra Bladet*'s correspondent in Moscow, and teaching students at a journalism school there.

The rigmarole was impressive in 2006. In a catch-22, I needed proof of hotel payment in order to get a visa; but payment was a complicated matter, and Inturist required a wire transfer to an obscure bank in Luxembourg(!). I followed all instructions, some of them bizarre, but the Russian tourism apparatus seemed to outsmart itself, as from Tsarist or Stalinist times. A ready traveler with hard currency, I found the whole thing just too macaronic, and cancelled the trip—until the day of departure, when my passport and visa just appeared on my desk at the U.S. Embassy. To this day I don't know how they got there.

The flight cancelled, I went to the Swiss Air counter downtown, and was able to rebook the flight. I left later the same evening.

I had always imagined Moscow to be exotic, culturally rich, interestingly threatening. It exceeded expectations. It could never have happened without Volodya's help and constant friendship. He drove me through the city, took me to the Moscow Music Conservatory, advised me on how to get around on the metro and tram. I saw the Noviy Arbat for blini and vodka, and was very happy with it all.

On one little car transfer, Volodya made an illegal left turn, and police were upon him from out of nowhere. I recognized the gambit as something that would happen in Cameroon. Russia was, of course, a more sophisticated place, and the police took him into a sort of mobile home where the transaction (AKA bribe) happened. When he came back to the car I asked him the amount he'd had to pay, and to the penny it was identical to the standard in Yaoundé: $25 U.S.

Volodya has been a close and reliable friend since I met in him in 1988. Here he is, December 22, at Østerport Station in Copenhagen, where he updated me on his latest scoops and plans. He was still dealing with the cold shoulder of some Danish colleagues and media bosses, but making his way by dint of good leads, lots of phone call follow-up, and Internet work late into the night.

Hard-hitting journalists are the monks of our time, uncompromising, socially removed while also keeping society literate and alive through the latter's hard times and long periods of mendacity and lost manuscripts. Many find them odd, but know somewhere within that they are needed, to keep track of errant egos, and to check the basest of human schemes, for our own good.

And a Third Russian

January 1, 2013

S'Novym Godom. Happy New Year.

Ilya Levin wandered into my office in 2008. He was looking for a posting in Africa, and I said, "Just fine."

Ilya wanted to tell me about some dark history of a previous assignment, but I wasn't interested.

"Are you an available bidder?" I asked. And yes he was, so onward to the U.S. Embassy in Dar-es-Salaam, as Public Affairs Officer in Tanzania.

Xenophobia marks the culture of the U.S. Department of State, where it is least needed. Others questioned my judgment and action. Ilya did fine; in fact his assignment was triumphant. In summer of 2010 I received a call on my cell phone in Conakry, Guinea, marked "highly urgent" on the screen. It was Ilya, calling to tell me he was happy in Dar.

Most correct: happiness is a matter of rarity and urgency when it happens. There is so little of it to go around.

Erudite and maybe a touch naïve, Ilya had been Amnesty International's local rep in Leningrad in the 1970s. Wearing a target on his back, he frequented the Writers Club where thinkers (i.e., enemies of the State) gathered.

He was a refusenik from 1975 to 1977. In 1977, the KGB tried out new technologies on him, and found a way of planting toxic powder to burn the flesh of a person's legs and buttocks seated on a certain chair. Ilya's leg went on fire and began to atrophy. The Leningrad Military Medical Academy—not in sync with their own internal security apparatus—stepped in and cured him of his flesh meltdown. Such were the ways of the experimentally-adventurous Soviet authorities. He testified about these bizarreries later at the Sakharov hearings in the U.S. Senate, 1978. As Levin says today, "The KGB works to cripple you and the military treats the injury."

The Soviet authorities spat him out like a bad tooth in 1977, so he went to the University of Texas at Austin, then to work at Voice of America in Washington, 1982-93. Then he joined USIA Director Charles Wick's WORLDNET overseas television network 1993-98. Finally, after 16 years, he made his way across the street to the U.S. Information Agency and acquired U.S. diplomatic status.

He was sent to Moscow, Vladivostok, Ashgabat, and Asmara, where he established Eritrea's first children's library. He kept his Russian accent and made bootleg vodka in the bathtub from a still-secret recipe, including elements of horseradish and hot jalapeño. His brand first appeared on the printed menu of the Petrovich eatery in Moscow in 2000. You can get it there to this day.

Eritreans loved him but didn't know what to make of him. They called him "The Russian." Shortly after Ilya got his posting to Tanzania and entered Swahili class at the Foreign Service Institute, he invited me up to his flat in Columbia Plaza for a drink. In the hallway on the way, he said, "I should warn you, the apartment is more a warehouse than a dwelling."

Indeed it was. The standard one-bedroom was stacked to the ceiling with books in cardboard cartons, with barely room enough for a tiny round table, two folding chairs, some Turkmen rugs rolled up, and a couple of bottles of spirits. We had fine whiskey and talked into the evening. Talk is everything to a Russian, a sign of friendship and acceptance. I was honored to be the interlocutor.

Ilya represented the U.S. government in Iraq in 2005-06, and has gone back to the region, now in a scrappy provincial area in eastern Afghanistan, where his ex-compatriots made some mischief in 1979. As U.S. diplomat, he is the senior civilian representative at a Polish military base in Ghazni, in southeastern Afghanistan.

Given the choice of learning Pashto or Dari a year ago, he energetically chose Dari, "the language of kings and of Omar Khayyam." He threw himself into it. He likes it there, and wants to spend an extra year.

In summer of 2008, Ilya traveled to San Miguel Allende in Mexico, and found the cocoa beans and recipe for perfect oven-baked chocolate. Here is a man who has his head screwed on right. I trust he wouldn't be offended if I called him the world's most benign eccentric. Eccentrics are our best and last hope, in a period of gridlock, global warming, and grey prose.

In an interview with the *Moscow Times* in 2000, he said, "Good vodka is nothing without friends to appreciate it."

Looking forward to our next drink and soirée, when Ilya has his next R&R in Washington, I hope, next spring.

Emperors' Clothes

January 8, 2013

Good news: December 29 no one was injured as the Central Market in Port-au-Prince burned down. Bad news: the market burned down. January 6, another fire – this one probably from arson – downed the Marché Public de Tabarre, J-B Aristide's old neighborhood. Is this not misfortune enough?

Haiti hardly has an excess of textiles or *prêt-à-porter*, let alone extras to shed, in yet another episode of its friends' incompetence. Deborah Sontag's December 23 article in *The New York Times* calls for response and consideration for sidelining the bitter-enders who once again have trivialized and mismanaged Haiti's people and problems.

March 31, 2010, Secretary Clinton convened a "donors' conference" in New York, where billions were pledged—but never spent—to restore an already fractured country after the earthquake of January 12. To date, $7.5 billion has been "disbursed" (assigned to contractors), but only a fraction actually paid out. The United States dithered for over a year to commit $65 million for housing, but to date only contracts have been signed, and little work commenced. With paltry results and 200-350,000 Haitians still in temporary camps, three years of dilatory and ineffectual chatter may now be enough. One billion dollars remain in the U.S. Treasury unspent, as well as $500 million of Global Red Cross funds (want to send another ten dollars to them over SMS, as you did in 2010?)

Doctors without Borders spent 58 percent of its $135 million on overhead. Only one percent of all humanitarian aid (ten percent of $2.2 billion) was entrusted to the government of Haiti. The U.S. spent six times more money ($1.2 billion) on temporary housing than the only $315 million permanent housing ("disbursed," not spent!)

By summer 2010, the Interim Haiti Reconstruction Commission (IHRC), chaired by Bill Clinton and Haitian then-prime minister Jean-Max Bellerive, raised only ten percent of the amount pledged to it. It was disbanded a year later, after just six meetings. The Haiti Reconstruction Fund, to be administered by the World Bank, never really got off the ground either.

The Clinton Bush Haiti Fund, the Clinton Foundation, and the American Red Cross fell short of their goals. So did Catholic Relief Services. Oxfam said in early 2011 that the IHRC and non-profits were equipped neither with staff or technical capacity. Why weren't Haitian voices heard?

In 2010, Secretary Clinton's counselor took it upon herself to cut off funding for Haiti's education sector, saying the United States would concentrate on four areas of reconstruction and development. Howls of protest erupted from Haiti's diaspora community, but they were stiff-armed and disregarded. After three years of lost opportunity—and donor fatigue all over—may we now ask why?

Haitians reside in a dysfunctional country, but they are not clueless. Refusal to hear them is hurtful and materially wasteful. Dabblers with bizarre developmental theories should not be entrusted forever to address a nation's despair. It would be time to remove and name and holders of these purses. Better yet, stop the pretense and just announce that foreign donors have no real intentions of reconstructing this broken nation, and remove unfulfilled IOUs from the table. Haitians would do better for themselves, without the empty promises of their bungling partners. Let January 12, 2013, be a time for exposure, and reversion to Haitians themselves of the tools and resources of their reconstruction.

Time to call out Haiti's faux friends, and put them back on the rack. Two former U.S. presidents took the mantle of these various endeavors, ignored Haitians' efforts to provide planning input, and now after three years should be judged on the results.

Inauguration Transfiguration

January 20, 2013

A flashback or, you might say, a relapse. Anyway, it's a true story.

January 1985: My little non-profit had been contracted to bring thirty exotic visitors from as many countries to attend Ronald Reagan's second inauguration. The idea had been cooked up by Charles Z. Wick, President Reagan's trusted friend, who boasted of having Thanksgiving dinner every year with the first family.

Wick was the director of the U.S. Information Agency, which was smothered under its pillow October 1, 1999. But 1985 was a good year.

My non-profit was tasked with getting the thirty visitors into the inauguration, scheduled for January 20. Slight hitch: the Republican National Committee wasn't forthcoming in providing tickets to the event. Those valued objects were set aside for party loyalists and domestic U.S. friends who could not be dissed. I well understood and would have done the same myself.

I told my boss that our project would calamitize if we weren't able to get tickets to the event. My boss called the little front office people of the little USIA to implore them: "You asked that we give front row seats to our international visitors' trip, financed by the U.S. government. You, therefore, provide the little tickets and we will do the rest."

Request denied. Mr. Wick, who preferred to be called "Wick," had too much to do that week, and friends to placate.

Thirty pretty important people were traveling 200,000 miles collectively for the event and would be annoyed if they could not have a look. We appealed, but NYET.

I made other arrangements: a briefing on the three branches of U.S. government, some visits to party headquarters, and I think a drop-in at the Air and Space Museum. As an afterthought, in those days before "Internet" was a known word and hand-helds were a fiction from Buck Rodgers cartoons, I booked a meeting room at the then-Dupont Plaza hotel, with—ka-ching—a television screen just in case.

I went to bed January 19 in my little condo on R Street in Washington, imagining painless forms of hara-kiri and considering the dramatic forms as well, so as possibly to go out in style and with people remembering me.

I turned on the radio news at 11:00 p.m. and got BBC London. *Mirabile dictu*, they said from London that the temperatures in Washington, DC, were so abnormally low that the public inauguration ceremony was to be cancelled, with a little private swearing-in as the back-up plan. Supreme Court Chief Justice Warren Burger was to swear in the president, with George H.W. Bush as understudy for Defender of the Free World.

I didn't quite know what to make of this. I knew it was cold because I was in Washington. But news of the change was coming from 3,675 miles (5,915 kilometers) away. I suspended plans for self-immolation.

The next day was pretty aggressively cold, around zero degrees

Fahrenheit. I met my group midday in the Dupont Plaza, and they were grateful not to have to go out. The ceremony had truly been canceled as a public event (imagine all the disappointed ticket-holders) and only television cameras and a handful of Extremely Very Important People (EVIPs) managed to be present.

My group of internationals got an exponentially better view of the swearing-in than the many thousands who hoped to be eyewitnesses. Mine were happy, and Devil take the Others.

My moment of demonstrated disgrace and disappointment was put off to another day. The Angel of Death hovered over my head and moved on to the next, deciding to spare me.

And by the way: Senator William Proxmire (D-WI) bestowed the Golden Fleece award on the inauguration, which that year cost the U.S. taxpayer $15.5 million. Previous honorable mentions went to a Department of Education grant of $219,592 for a curricular package "to teach college students how to watch television," a $97,000 project by the National Institute of Mental Health to study what takes place in Peruvian brothels, and $103,000 to the National Science Foundation to "compare aggressiveness in sunfish that drink tequila instead of gin."

I was proud—let's say relieved—to benefit from one of 168 Golden Fleece awards (1975-88), and went forth to formulate such inventive modules as this blog posting.

Remembering Todman

August 18, 2014

The August 17 *Washington Post* carries a fine obit on Terence A. Todman, deceased August 13.

No quibbles with Emily Langer's synthesis of this remarkable man, my first boss in 1986 in the Foreign Service. Just a few footnotes to add:

I was Ambassador Todman's press officer the day he gave his fateful news conference in Copenhagen, denying that his future posting would be South Africa. He had to set the record straight, as the Scandinavian press was buzzing with rumors that he would be Ronald Reagan's man in Pretoria, half a decade before Nelson Mandela was released from Robben Island. African-descended Todman played his cards close to his chest, but was heard at the office to say, "They won't play that game with me," referring to what would have been a connivance of tokenism had he accepted the job. Edward J. Perkins went for the bait that Todman turned down, making his own personal decision to do so. Perkins, too, was a diplomat in a squeeze, and chose a route as honorable as Todman's, though in another direction.

Scandinavians loved Todman, and the media loved him most of all. They loved him partly for his origins in a former Danish colony (Saint Thomas), but more because of his lively wit and the steadfastness of his ideas and beliefs. They disagreed with a lot of what he said, but never doubted the sincerity or the refinement of his arguments. They teased and taunted him, and he gave as good as he got.

Todman was something of a conservative, though as a thinking human being was not a "pure" anything. He fully believed in Reagan's Strategic Defense Initiative ("Star Wars") and pressed the point at every opportunity. No free lunches at his residence: he sparred, challenged, and held his ground with all invited groups when probably not a single Scandinavian saw things as he did, especially after the Reykjavik talks faltered over this single issue in October of 1986.

Remember, Scandinavia was a linchpin in the final years of the Cold War: NATO-loyal Norway, perplexed Denmark, neutral Sweden, and scrappy Finland were key, very close to the Warsaw Pact countries, and were courted by both super powers in those decisive years.

I transcribed the press conference referred to in Emily Langer's obit. Todman's future was big news in Scandinavia, and the press room at the embassy swarmed with more journalists than I had ever seen before in a single place. I was nervous about Todman saying the "right" things that day. He was just back from two weeks in Washington, on a visit he called a "vacation." Everyone knew there was more to it than that. He never told his staff exactly what happened, but everyone knew what the Reagan Administration's intentions were, and that Todman had been offered the Big Post in Pretoria and had turned it down.

Todman ad-libbed for well over an hour that day. I've never seen quite the skill, before or since, on the part of a diplomat of any country. He went on at some length about the virtues of Reagan's anti-apartheid stance ("constructive engagement" in those days), and spoke with a mastery and intensity unhindered by detectable signs of emotion.

And yes, he really did say, "Once we have a policy that has credibility...then we can start thinking of who is the very best person to go to South Africa." I remember. I transcribed it.

Some ice water of panic went through my veins as he embedded this nugget in an otherwise favorable depiction of Reagan's South Africa policy. Had it slipped out of his mouth unintentionally? Could he ever backtrack? I remember thinking, "Nordic gods, let that one phrase be forgotten, or the White House will have Todman's head on a pike." Out of protection for him, I wanted to excise the phrase from the transcript, but I knew I couldn't, since the Scandinavian media had recorded the whole thing. Banner headlines the next morning in all Scandinavian capitals said, "Diplomat says U.S. policy toward South Africa lacks credibility" ("*mangler trovaerdighed*"). This was a slight distortion of the words he really used, but the gist was there.

I think the White House was apoplectic, but silently so.

I dreaded coming to work the next day, but Todman had the time of his life, giving a single red rose to each female member of the embassy staff while singing James Brown's "*I feel gooood....*" He had said what was needed, while artfully inserting a key phrase with a wink for the Scandinavian press. He knew his press better than his advisors did, including me. This was the relationship he had built up over two years with those who loved his ability to say what he thought and not what his interlocutors or bosses thought he should say.

Lesson learned: never betray the Master, but do as you must. It will work out in the long run.

Todman kept a silently vindictive White House in check. He knew his comment would bring wrath, but knew also that as a rare African American ambassador, he could not be tossed overboard, not with domestic politics so much a part of foreign policy. Also, he could say he was misquoted, and that his actual words were not actionable. Stymied, the White House kept him in limbo for some months. Not knowing how to handle him, they let him stay on for almost half a year extra.

Todman had the kryptonite of Congressional Black Caucus to protect him. After dithering a few months, the Reagan White House relented to pressure, and named him to Argentina, where in time he convinced the Argentine government to open their archives on Nazi immigrants to the country; he also talked them into pegging the troubled Argentine currency to the U.S. dollar, which gave that fitful economy a bit of respite in their eternal struggle to establish a credible peso. These days they are not so lucky.

In the course of time, I wrote to Todman to commend him on these achievements, and said they seemed to bear his fingerprints. In his letter back to me he said teasingly, "What would give you that impression?"

After he retired, Todman was picked by the Bush White House to do some freelancing, to settle the intractable problems in Haiti's dysfunctional domestic politics. Someone must have thought, "He's of African descent and from the Caribbean, so he must know something about the place."

He didn't, was clueless about Haiti, and made the same errors as his lame predecessors from both U.S. political parties. Surely he might have realized that Haiti is of a different galaxy from any neighboring island. He should have avoided the sugary trap all the others had fallen into.

Second lesson learned: best not to try to repeat a perfect performance.

I never had a better teacher than Terence Todman. I couldn't ever refer to this complex man and selfless mentor by his first name as others do casually, not even in the recesses of my private mind. But today I break the pattern just once and say, "Goodbye Terry, and go well."

Thought's Colors
August 25, 2014

There we go, forty years almost to the day, when I registered in a seminar with John Hawkes in Providence. *The New York Times* of August 24 cites these seminars somewhat playfully in its book review section.

Then as now, "creative writing" seemed an indulgence when it tried to be an academic discipline, something for the leisured classes. The difference in 1974 was that, with a bit of academic aid, it came for free if you were willing to drive a taxi to make ends meet. I did. Financial persecution of students today makes this unimaginable.

People called John Hawkes "Jack." He certainly was accessible and friendly, but I called him "John Hawkes." He wrote marvelous prose, a bit dark and impenetrable, one novel a year like a planned litter of pups. Like Jerry Lewis, he was highly respected in France, more so than in his native United States.

Hawkes used to say, "It's not that I teach in order to write books, I write books to be able to keep my teaching job." Novelists didn't make much money those days, unless they were William Styron or Normal Mailer.

That year, 1974, Richard Nixon gave me the best birthday present ever by resigning from office. Good riddance, and on to Brown for a utopian autumn, though with uncertainty all around. No jobs, no prospects. Might as well be back in school. Being a taxi driver required only a driver's license and evidence of not having a police record. I wasn't much more qualified as a driver than as a writer.

I plodded with my not-so-good novel that fall, turning in one chapter each week. Most of the others in the class had serious writer's block, and showed up empty-handed to Hawkes's hospitable living room near the campus, where he held his classes. By October he became pretty exasperated, formulating his thoughts gently but saying in effect, "If you are unable to write anything, even a paragraph, how is it you registered for this course?"

My novel was not cited in "American Masterpieces," but when he said, "one chapter per week," I thought he meant it. So did the others in the class, but they were just paralyzed. No nostalgia for those troubled times. My work was never digitized, so I can hope you will never see it.

Everything those days was a matter of "finding one's voice." I thought then, and still do, that my voice is somewhere in my throat. I think I know what Hawkes and others were driving at with this trendy endeavor, but it sounded esoteric to me. I didn't have a southern drawl or the abbreviated neologisms of an immigrant; I just sort of talked.

He had us dictate anecdotes on a device known then as a "tape recorder." Then we compared the transcriptions of what we actually said, to the fashioned prose we realized would sound more "natural." The point was, producing a spontaneous, written passage was not a simple matter of saying what came into your head. The word "flow" was not permitted in our discussions, and in fact doesn't mean much. The recordings made it clear that there was some work involved in construing spontaneity for the reader. Good point.

John Hawkes was one of an Athenian cluster of lofty minds in Providence those days—Alan Trueblood, Edwin Honig, others.

As Proust would say startlingly in one of his lengthy sentences describing the battlefields of the Great War, "blah blah, now all of them dead, each one: dead."

The intellect has its way of carrying on, as the standard of the fallen is taken up by survivors. Global climate change so far notwithstanding, it throws itself forward. Needs of the stomach, the groin, disputes in the gut between malignancy and invisible antibodies coming to our rescue even as we serve as their hosts—all come as disturbance and demonstrate astonishing balance. Nature, which imposes these needs on us, seems to have no obligation to satisfy them. But endowed with intellect, we can hope to arrange these things for ourselves. Sometimes we evoke cravings as prose, as messages in a bottle, seeking assistance from idealized people and imagined tastes. But we learn soon enough that mentioning them does little to calm them. This yields recipes, erotica, and medical dictionaries, all of them pretty far removed from what really happens on a given day.

Lots of discussion these days of something called "genius," as if we could produce it by defining it. Lone thought? Communal? Can't teach it, I think, any more than "creative writing." I do not disdain the discipline, but even with the amiable and persistent efforts of John Hawkes, it didn't seem to leap from one host to another by contiguity. The current fad of trying to define and explain it will soon pass.

Brown, 250 years back, as noted in the *Times* of August 24. John Hawkes, niche folk hero in France and respected but little read in his own country—back just forty. Markers matter. Reminders bring us back to what once made sense.

Like digits (I mean, zero and one) the intellect can have a limited shelf life in an individual and may be deleted by a sunspot. However, so far it keeps ticking, like an obstinate heart, until it stops, soon enough to be replaced by another. The groin and the gut will carry on as they must. With health and balance (Greek philosophers said things about this) and luck keeping malignancy in check, the three will overlap and keep themselves going.

John Hawkes understood these things, but wasn't very successful in teaching them. I'm heartened that someone remembers him. It is always time to take up his cloudy, haunting novels once again, stories around the campfire.

Believing is Seeing

September 14, 2014

September 10, President Obama rolled out his new anti-IS intentions. Meanwhile two high-octane intellects separately discussed their appraisals of Obama's foreign policy. I won't say "tautology," but each made perfect sense in its own framework, each might have frayed if confronted with the other. I would say, "It would have been fascinating to have them in the same room," but I am not into reality TV.

With the recent Rice suspension and the NFL now possibly on its way down, a likely new American national sport (little league) might be Quarterbacking Obama's Foreign Policy – the A League bashing it, the B league supporting it. Mainly a spectator sport and for intellectuals only.

A couple of years ago, Kurt Campbell, Obama's previous Assistant Secretary for State for East Asia and Pacific Affairs, came up with the word "pivot" for a reorienting of energies to the Pacific. He has repented ever since, saying, "Please call it a 'rebalance.'" He spoke with Chicago communitarianist Amitai Etzioni at the George Washington University campus September 8. He said (I paraphrase),

"The United States never left Asia and never will. The challenge is to get domestic U.S. politics to understand and support this."

A day later, Vali Nasr, dean of the Johns Hopkins School of Advanced International Studies (SAIS), said to his counterpart James Goldgeier at American University's School of International Service (paraphrase again), "If only we had a Richard Holbrooke, things might be better," referring to ominous developments in the Middle East and surroundings.

Campbell would be primarily in the B (Obama Yes) League of the new sport, Nasr in the A (Obama No) League. Both were cautious and mindful enough to cite arguments contrary to their own, and even give some credence to them. But as camouflage, these citations did not go very far. Each argument remained pretty contained within itself, pretty irrefutable, and I'm afraid adding little to our knowledge of the world at this perilous time. Imagine Galileo's Vatican saying, "But on the other hand…" I don't think so. The walls pressed in on poor, outflanked Galileo. Today's reasoning goes in a similar fashion, building impressive constructs based on certain major premises. Take 'em or leave 'em, but don't try removing them. The stakes (pardon the pun) are now intellectual prestige rather than death by fire, which is out of favor at the moment in Washington.

Seeing and hearing these brilliant displays makes living in Washington worthwhile, despite the prices and traffic anger. Like Twain with smoking, I have sworn off them "many times," but never managed to stay away for long.

Campbell and Nasr are both great thinkers. No issues with that. Both span theory and practice ably. Both impressively speak without notes. It's just that the reference points skip around serpent-like, so you can't get a fair shot at them. A lot has to do with the unarticulated nature and mood of the speaker. Some people are just born cheerful.

Kurt Campbell clearly has affection and deep knowledge of Asia, and a personal investment in finding ways to let both sides complement and benefit each other. He had full support of President Obama in trying to make this happen, and he may succeed even in the face of the John Mearsheimers of this world, predicting inevitable conflict as countries become great powers. Nothing is inevitable anymore, and shame on Mearsheimer and adulators like Robert Kaplan.

Campbell had the perfect interlocutor in the great Amitai Etzioni, who has been advocating something called "Mutually Assured Restraint" for this and other flashpoints, and why not.

Nasr, just the following day, likewise had the gentle and very informed prodding of NATO specialist Goldgeier, who graciously encouraged students to join the dialogue.

My issue is with Nasr's blunt and facile rejection of Obama's efforts and actions, as if Obama were the *deus* behind the terrible *ex machina* we have to deal with in the world today. There were antecedents, which Nasr artfully acknowledges. Presidents no longer have such freedom of action as before, and thank the gods for the 1973 War Powers Act which makes it so. But when Nasr pines for the Holbrooke days of the Dayton Accords halting the genocide in the Balkans, he establishes a strange premise: the "If Only" School of Foreign Policy. If only Holbrooke could be replaced by another Holbrooke. Let's see: if Beethoven and Faulkner had died (my understanding is that they did), who should or could replace them? The times, the circumstances, are not comparable. I, too, am a Holbrooke admirer, but I wouldn't judge today's practitioners by their ability or inability to reincarnate themselves as him.

Campbell's "Why Not" School appeals a little more to me, but we are not buying refrigerators here. Good research calls for persuasion, but we would be better off with less of the latter. Foreign policy does not exist for the happiness of the observer. It is as cancer is to the oncologist: the reason to go on, and mostly a source of anguish to those affected.

I think Nasr exaggerates when he attributes to Obama the idea that "less foreign policy is better for us." That is a bit of a cheap shot. Leaning towards membership in the B League myself, I think it's reductionist to say that Obama is "passing the buck" to let Iraqis "settle" Iraq. The alternatives, please? Nasr's concession to Obama's success in dealing with Iran is not exactly disingenuous, but it does serve the purpose of getting his harsh message easier to swallow. His comparison of Obama's foreign policy to "the drunk looking for his keys where the light is, not where he left them," is irresistible. But I don't know how it increases our understanding of the scary circumstances we must deal with, or else.

Arguments are not really arguments until they are challenged by able opponents. And yet, opposition is not the virtue here, fuller comprehension is. Today's Washingtonian gets ahead by drawing attention to elegant but simplified views of what ticks, so that people can identify you as a "Kissingerian," or a "Mearsheimerist." This formation of Schools produced the impressive style, and hollow content, of political debate in France in the 1950s and 60s. We can do better.

Reacting to the beheading of James Foley, AU Prof Michael Brenner said in his own op/ed of August 25, "The flood of commentary, as usual, reveals little in the way of rigorous logic but much in the way of disjointed thinking and unchecked emotion…The country would be well served if our leaders observed a moratorium on public statements for several days…and devoted themselves to some concentrated hard thinking."

Go, Brenner.

What all seem to agree on is that perceptions are everything, and s/he who can mold and guide them gets to rule the roost.

A Class Act from Bangui

September 21, 2014

With worthy competition, the Central African Republic (CAR) may be the most miserable place on earth. Twelve per cent of its population is displaced, eight per cent are refugees in other countries, 54 per cent urgently need humanitarian assistance, 30 per cent of its schools and hospitals have been destroyed in recent conflicts, 7,000 children kidnapped, and the per capita income has fallen from $461 in 2008 to $294 in 2014.

Much of the violence in the past year has been Christian on Muslim, defying the paradigm some have come to expect. At least four terrorist groups wander freely in the borders of this former empire (remember Bokassa?). After four decades of instability, the country basically imploded in 2012.

No one expected much other than the stifled cries of the suffering from out of this doomed place, but interim President Catherine Samba-Panza spoke at the Brookings Institution September 19, and gave an out-of-the-ballpark talk to an inquiring audience. Remarkable how an individual can give a face to abstractions like countries and their peoples.

President Samba-Panza speaks like a Sorbonne professor, in measured tones and nuance. She plays no games, gives no embellishments or hyperboles.

Urged by a delegation of women in early 2014, the then-mayor of Bangui, the country's capital, presented herself to something called the "National Transition Council." In a state of near-total breakdown, the country had nothing much other than the NTC as a tiny entity of organization and sovereignty. The country has borders, after all, even if no one much heeds them.

The NTC agreed to give Catherine Samba-Panza a try, partly because no one much else was foolhardy enough to take on such a task. There wasn't much competition for the job.

Her plan was pretty understandable, with massive if unlikely goals: dialogue, tolerance, reconciliation. CAR is surrounded on every side but one, by neighboring countries which export disorder and chaos in the region. Militias, terrorists, jihadists, gangsters. Not a good neighbor with the sole exception of Cameroon to the west.

In July 2014, Interim President Samba-Panza called for a "Reconciliation Forum" in neighboring Brazzaville, and got sign-on from countries in the region, including some which did not attend the forum. Empty statements of intent? Well, statements may work better than silence and misanthropy.

Speaking with the serenity of a sovereign, the president said at Brookings, "I granted authority to MINUSCA" (The UN peacekeeping mission in CAR is now at 45 per cent of its personnel target and yet is able to pacify somewhat a restless and terrified public, even with only 2,000 troops).

President Samba-Panza, citing Ebola, regional terrorism, and economic and social dislocation as major distractions, noted that ninety NGOs have rallied to the assistance of CAR, and that improvement has come *"petit à petit."* No major claims here, just an update on how hell can incrementally turn into something slightly better.

"Quelque chose a déclenché," the president said, affirming that a vicious cycle may just be going into reverse, where all want it. Jihad-

ists and Christians, abusers on all sides are sitting together in some instances, talking their way out of an impasse which works against all.

Perhaps only a woman can make such things happen. Samba-Panza is the first woman of any authority to lead a francophone African country, and the third on the continent. The "plan" is to allow CAR's people first to go through the mourning process, then mutual forgiveness, then peace. Simplistic? Utopian? What lesser goal could suffice?

She says she will not be a candidate in the elections she seeks to establish in 2015. Any Washington audience finds such affirmations energizing, possibly unlikely after five decades of the doomed empires of the Men-Who-Wouldn't-Let-Go now stifling Africa's growth and well-being. Away, away with all of them.

A skeptic from Burkina Faso asked the president, "In that case, what is your advice to Blaise Compaoré [the president of the former Upper Volta, whose presidential "term" reads "1987-" as if to infinity, like the others leading their countries to perdition]"?

Interim President Samba-Panza did not rise to the bait. With poise she said, "I am only setting an example in my country. What happens in Burkina Faso is a matter for the people of Burkina Faso to decide." You had to be there to sense the buzz in the room.

One Western diplomat said that Catherine Samba-Panza's presentation might raise unrealistic expectations for her broken country. Fair enough, but how to realize expectations other than to have them?

Safety in Numbers
October 13, 2014

I don't mean it in a smarmy way: everything is numbers these days, it just is. Undergraduates looking for a pretty sustainable livelihood should become "M&E" specialists—monitoring and evaluation. If I were a donor I, too, would want to know what I am getting for my money.

An established magnet for Washington intelligentsia, the Center for Global Development pulled in yet another fine gathering, this time October 9. They got onto their premises the president of the African Development Bank, a director of development data group in the World Bank, and a VP of the Bill and Melinda Gates Foundation (Donald Kaberuka, Haishan Fu, and Mark Suzman, respectively.) The occasion was the launching of something called the "Data Revolution," as outlined in a new study cosponsored by CGD and the African Population and Health Research Center.

Hyperboles like "revolution" are useful in getting our heads twisted in useful new ways, and in getting people into a room.

In the development field, data collection has been a pretty dreary exercise in recent decades, used to vilify or lionize a given project but not often enough put to the service of policy and program development. The idea here is to exit the blame and praise business and get down to some serious planning, especially in places where projects and policies have come up with disappointing results. A bit parallel to the way think tanks in general abandoned their perches of pure analysis in the 1970s and since, so as to (duh!) influence policy before it became a fly pinned to cardboard, only to be entered into a taxonomy of past success and failure. Use the efforts, rather, to model the future.

It's heartening to see the World Bank, the Bill and Melinda Gates Foundation, and the African Development Bank (AfDB) all using the same language and seeing a similar way forward. None too soon for publics and donors weary of the sorts of anecdotes which would close the spigots of finance and efforts. The world's suffering will not vanish if we play peek-a-boo with it. Failures notwithstanding, problems need solutions in a demographically-exploding and interconnected world; our survival may depend on them. Getting it wrong a thousand times is not a reason to give up the effort, since the consequences are humanitarian crises, resource wars, and terrorism. Jeffrey Sachs' solutions of doubling the amount of wasted resources will not get us anywhere, but neither will denial. There's no alternative to getting it right in developing countries.

The data "revolution" comes from a multilateral bank's recognition of a Senegalese taxi driver's analysis, "On ne mange pas la croissance" ["You can't eat growth"]. AfDB President Kaberuka put it up on the screen behind him at the October 9 presentation, I think because he gets it. Large organizations can filter data to make stasis look like "progress," and can show encouraging data when the average citizen has gotten nothing, but nothing, from the process.

Any observer knows this. That the multilaterals are stating their understanding of it shows we may have hope in sustaining their efforts. Obscene overheads and overpaid consultants—and organizational distance from the supposed beneficiaries of their programs—get the ridicule and contempt they deserve. But turning our backs on needy populations will only aggravate conditions for all.

Who asks the questions in the field? What trust is given to the interlocutor by the skeptical village inhabitant, and for what motive? As President Kaberuka said logically, an increase of one dollar a day for the northern Ugandan, compared to the city dweller in Johannesburg, doesn't mean much. Some of the data sets that have passed for "growth" are just silly.

More relevantly, even if data were used more rationally to formulate development policies and programs, who would even be able to pull it off? No one knows, though some leap farther on faith than others.

Mark Suzman of the Bill and Melinda Gates Foundation rightly mocks the new "Strategic Development Goals" of the World Bank (the roll-over of the Millennium Development Goals (MDGs) to hit a "maturity" point in 2015). Referring to the greatly expanded numbers of criteria from eight in 2000 to over 160 in 2015, he calls them, "No Target Left Behind." The cause for encouragement is to see World Bank and AfDB officials chuckling along with him. Philanthropy can cite the name that multilaterals dare not speak, but now the sectors appear to collaborate as they had not done before.

John Podesta, Counselor to the U.S. President these days, says that private sector investors are pounding on the door of the United Nations to be in on the Strategic Development Goals, where they mainly fled or hid under the table from the MDGs. They understand that investments in risky circumstances pay off only when there is some sort of infrastructure, rule of law, reliable water and electricity, and minimal security—goals which were multilaterals' and do-gooders' specialties until the private sector woke up following the 2008 economic crisis. This alone qualifies as something of a revolution.

AfDB President Kaberuka pretty much stole the show October 9, and played on Mark Twain by referring to "Lies, Damned Lies, and GDP"—indicating that gross domestic product just doesn't measure much that affects the lives of ordinary people. U.S. GDP includes the money spent in cleaning up oil spills and digging out from hurricanes and snowstorms. As an indicator, it is pretty outmoded.

Data Revolution Project Director Amanda Glassman summed it up well in her comment, "Data is only as good as its use." Again, I don't know if this is a "revolution," and it's one of those intuitive truths that any average Joe could explain to a PhD in data collection. Maybe not for the first time, we have institutional awareness, humility, and reorienting, and I'm relieved. I may become a willing U.S. taxpayer after all.

Gone but Not Forgotten
December 31, 2014

I want to say how very sorry I am about the Gulf Stream. I hope some Europeans and West Africans will be there to accept my heartfelt apology.

We had original claim to the Gulf Stream, in fact. It did come from us, and one of ours figured it out: Benjamin Franklin, by following the printed coastal weather reports in 18th-century newspapers in the colonies.

When we began the Experiment in the late 1940s, our goal was to extend the productive capacity of the Earth, not limit or disrupt it. The recently declassified documents, "Global Weather Change for Peace," indicate that we had the best minds on it, and a couple of theologians as well. Admittedly Reinhold Niebuhr wasn't on board, but we got a couple of others.

Repentant Nazis worked with us, it is true. But their intentions were honorable. They never lied to us when they said they would kill us, nor did they when then said they wanted to make up for their uncles' misdeeds. The documents confirm this.

Our goals were relatively modest at first, to see if we could grow pine forests in the Bight of Benin and papayas in the Orkneys. Just to see, you understand. If you've never had a papaya straight from the tree, you can't know the blessing it is. Mankind deserved a better chance to have these pleasures firsthand. All we did was muster the resources to make it happen.

We weren't naïve; we knew Global Weather Change for Peace could cause desertification and erratic weather patterns, but the Boolean coefficient had the risk low to an acceptable two per cent plus change.

I know what you are thinking: "Why didn't they quit when things started going wrong?"

I don't fault you for thinking this. The promise of success far outweighed the perils of failure. Plus, inquisitive boys needed to know what this might all lead to.

We pondered the awe of the program, further codenamed "Icarus," in the need-to-know form. We never meant to divert the thing; we only wanted to spruce it up a little.

So there has been some death and destruction, okay. But don't go around saying this wasn't your specialty during previous centuries. You first, then us. The big difference was, we did it for Peace. Plus it was our Gulf Stream to do with as we pleased.

By the turn of the current century we knew the variables were working against us. So we engaged the Office of Psychological Operations and renamed the project "El Niño" ("The Child"). We thought we might deflect some of the inquiring eyes to our Latin American friends. After all, they had taken in unrepentant Nazis (unlike ours) and deserved, well, a bit of a lesson.

The plan worked for about five years, until about 2004 when tsunamis got people as far away as Southeast Asia and the Indian Ocean. This was definitely not in our AOR (Area of Responsibility), so we truly think we should get a pass for that one.

Still, the variables persistently went against us. Snow in Mississippi, floods in East Anglia, what the fuck, this was just not fair and we can't be blamed for everything. Well, okay, the volcano in Iceland and the Bermuda Triangle, we'll take our shots for that. And, okay, the cod and tuna fleeing the Georges Bank also. But Mauritania gets a windfall of fish stocks off its coast, and you're welcome. Fish gotta swim, and we knew that. We made mistakes but eventually we own up to all of them. In that regard all you ever did was take, take. You never gave. Pfft!

In 2014, Europeans stepped forward and got a satellite to land on Mars. Way to go, and we support your efforts entirely.

In fact we were there on a low-footprint mission there in the 1960s ("Project Americans are from Mars"—*pace* Robert Kagan, who later plagiarized the name, or more properly "appropriated" it, since U.S. government concepts cannot be copyrighted). Early encounters were promising but we wanted to be magnanimous and let others seem to take the lead.

Problem was, when the European Mars probe hit the planet, the Martians gathered their children and made them stay inside until the batteries went dead.

They thought we were back again.

Ward Just and *American Romantic*

January 2, 2015

With a certain urgency, I write on Ward Just's eighteenth novel, *American Romantic*. It's about the stay anyone in the Foreign Service would want to write, but Just has done it for us. Gail Godwin in *The New York Times* of June 6 called it "one of his best."

"With urgency," because I am trying to recapture the marvels of its first half, before the sogginess of its second half gets the upper hand in my memory.

All people, and certainly Foreign Service Officers, want others to understand their lives and the risks they take, emotional and other. Humans believe their chronicles have value or interest, but fall short of articulating them adequately. Oral history, the written word, cinema just don't do it, I think because compressing a life into an explanation only reduces it and dry-packs it. Great art leaves the illusion that it's possible, but of course it's not really.

Just shows me my Washington as no one else, and any of us is always grateful for a good mirror, since anatomy does not allow us to look at ourselves.

Nothing is perfect. While I see the streets of my own past neighborhoods in Just's tight and expressive prose, the tiniest corruptions creep in—worldly Americans speaking their own language as if their prep schools had made them half-British (not), their quests to see minute elements of other lives' meanings, when many Washingtonians in fact are a couple of steps beyond bewilderment and, well, clueless.

As Emerson and Thoreau and Dreiser showed me "my" Boston, and Balzac "my" Paris, and Sherwood Anderson "my" Ohio, Just shows how the mind can echo, based on a place and type of character who could be ourselves.

Everyone loves an echo... echo... echo...

Harry Sanders, the hapless but intelligent and committed junior officer in *American Romantic* appeals to any Foreign Service Officer who has ever been junior. Duty calls. Gorgeous "tumbles" with exotic foreigners, emotional bungee jumping and permanent wounds, like Sanders's feet which take beating in an early chapter of the book and leave him on a walking cane for the rest of his life. This disfigurement is Shakespearean, like Richard III"s crooked spine. Richard, twisted; Sanders, wounded. Vulnerability is appealing in Just's characters.

My quibbles with *American Romantic* are minor. Anyone who has ever seen cinema, from *The Great Train Robbery* on, is aware that the lovely Siegelinde will reappear at some point after her perfect love in, then disappearance from, Harry's life. We don't really need memories of Berlin and the Brahms *Requiem* to set up those bowling pins near the end of the story. Also, we understand that Sanders's wife, May, comes well short of being a soulmate, though the point is made a bit flat-footedly and many times. And the perfect car accident releases the main character from his bondage when we want it even before he does. And not every well-achieving junior officer ends up with multiple ambassadorships in the U.S. system. But anyway...

These little flaws are well outweighed by the startling charms of this wonderful book.

Harry's mentor, the good-hearted Basso Earle III, is the boss anyone would want, and at some point we all meet him, even if only briefly. These people do exist. They are not cynics or screamers. Bravo, Just, for finding one to remind us of this.

George F. Kennan makes a hilarious cameo appearance at a Washington reception, remembered as "Kennel" by Harry Saunders's soul-pinched wife, May (By the way, where is Richard Holbrooke in the early Vietnam scenes of the book?).

Harry's genuine curiosity and dedication to the job are convincing, and he even knows a thing or two about world culture—not all that unusual in the real U.S. Foreign Service. Not all of us want or receive multiple ambassadorial appointments, but fair enough: some readers may think of individuals as "diplomats" only when they reach that stage. It reminds me of the Russian who asked me once in Denmark, "Do you expect to be a diplomat one day?

"I am a diplomat, actually."

"No, I mean, a *real* diplomat."

It's a virtue, not a vice, that Just builds the setting to respond to expectations of likely readers—the loyal house servant Ramon, the nightly whiskeys, the gradual loss of self by the one sent by fate to Asia, then Africa, then Norway, then the Balkans... In fact many of us learn to penetrate and rejoice at our multi-country assignments, but true enough, in reality *heimveh* (as Just would call it) does set in eventually and a natural tendency to see those around us as "locals" or "the others." Many (not all) Foreign Service Officers in fact go beyond those limits, develop real affections for the people and places they meet, whence "going native" and the system's way of uprooting FSOs regularly and predictably.

In praise of Just, his Harry traverses rites of passage and very dire predicaments. While we have not all mangled our feet escaping insurgents in the jungle, all FSOs have had moments of emotional peril and encounters with hostility.

The rare instances of pedagogy ("station chief," "Marine Security Guard," "CODEL," "Elysée") are agile enough. Though commonplaces for those in the business, they are welcome reference for those who benefit.

Foreign Service, Foreign Legion. How many of our good friends really think we have the credit ratings and internal computer systems of demiurges? Any reminder of our limits and our frailties is welcome.

There is only one Ward Just, and he spans the gap between easy fiction and the sometimes mystified world of Washington makers and shakers. *The Congressman Who Loved Flaubert*. The title, alone, of one of his earliest tales lifts stereotypes out of their straitjackets, while also reaffirming their existence.

Flaubert: "I am Emma Bovary."

Just: "I am Harry Sanders."

It would not be a crazy pretense for him to say so.

Woman in the Dunes

January 4, 2015

Tony Hervas, a colossus of a man, was chief U.S. interpreter (Spanish/English) during the lengthy negotiations reverting the Panama Canal "back" to Panama under President Carter.

His flawless precision and baritone voice worthy of Fischer-Dieskau were models we all emulated, but knew we could never match.

"We," that is, the fleet of interpreters dipping in and out of the Language Services Office of the State Department in the 1970s and 80s. None of us had real jobs, nor could we likely have held them down if we'd been given the chance. We were collectively restless, very chummy with one another, and living on youth's false illusion that youth might accompany us all the way through.

Tony knew better, and in a camouflaged sort of way really cared about us. He never would have admitted it.

He was patriarchal and kept his compassion and very good humor out of view.

I sat in his cubicle once in the Main State Department building, thinking he could never tell one of us from the others, when my eyes fell on a serious-looking poster opposite his desk: "Ten Steps in case of Nuclear Attack: one, avoid glass and mirrors; two, stay near to the floor…; ten, kiss your ass goodbye."

When I burst out laughing, Tony only looked at me knowingly, hardly smiling. I realized I'd never really known him, and probably never would. His achievements seemed unattainable by normal humans.

Six years after the rupture of diplomatic relations between the U.S. and Algeria in 1973, someone in CU, the exchanges office in the State Department, decided to take a big risk and bring eighty (80!) Algerian advanced students to the United States for a 30-day visit.

For the occasion, the Office of Language Services (LS) needed to haul in a dozen of us in a hurry to upgrade us from consecutive to simultaneous interpretation. I didn't think I was qualified, and said so to Tony.

"Just go in and take the test," she said. "For conference [the highest category], you have to be flawless. Not for seminar, though."

Lamb to slaughter, I went in for testing and came out with a new contract that doubled my daily rate on days when simultaneous was scheduled. It had all to do more with the extraordinary needs that week than with merit. But Tony always knew what he was doing. He never put anyone out there who couldn't do the work.

It's sort of hazy now, but I think I went straight from the test into a terrifying amphitheater in the Department, where the eighty Algerians (presumably future leaders of their country) were being briefed on U.S. Middle East policy. Imagine messing up any of this.

I was reassured to see interpreting booths up at the top of the room. This meant that the real pros would do their conference simultaneous through electronic equipment and earphones. I felt Death had passed me over.

Some of the famous "Arabists" in the State Department were briefing the group, whose very presence was a bold venture given shaky U.S.-Algerian relations at that time. These guys must have been DASs (Deputy Assistant Secretaries), but without context, I knew only that all hinged on perfect interpretation from their English to the visitors' French, on a sensitive topic.

I had entered the amphitheater *in medias res*, no context. Tony was standing at the top of the room, near the interpreters' booths, to oversee the whole thing.

When it came time for the elegant French to come tumbling out of those booths and into the earpieces of the visitors, there was a minor disturbance: the electronic system had gone dead. That is, dead. Fully staffed with the best French interpreters in the business, all for naught.

I knew what was expected. Microscopically small, I glanced up to Tony and very reluctantly pointed to myself and put my face in interrogation mode.

Unambiguously, Tony looked back at me and nodded "yes." Something about the shape of the amphitheater, and my helplessness in it, made me think of Hirohsi Teshigahara's *Woman in the Dunes*, which isn't much of a story. It shows a woman stuck in a sand pit and unable to climb out. Had seen the movie some years before, but now suddenly I understood it completely.

Preparing for the execution, I grabbed paper and pen, moved to the bottom of the amphitheater where the action was—down past the group of eighty—and sat by the DASs to do consecutive, phrase-by-phrase interpretation.

I realized as I took notes that I was so terrified that my throat had frozen from fear. I knew I could interpret the English to some form of accurate French, but I also knew after a few seconds that I wouldn't ever get a sound out. I looked up again at Tony, who nodded, "Yes, you."

When a pause came in the narrative, I scanned my notes but I realized I wouldn't even squeak when it came my turn to speak. The Algerians looked plenty annoyed to be in the pantheon of child-killing imperialists. This could have been my own projection, because they were behaving politely enough.

If it had been a film, the heartbeat would crescendo on the sound track, turning to timpani crashes.

My terror vanished as one of the DASs pushed me aside and took over seamlessly in French. I glanced at his colleagues, and all four indicated they had perfect French, and could do their briefing directly.

The Angel of Death came a second time to take me, and left in disgust.

Five years later, Tony had me once again in his office. He knew, better than I did, that a suitcase and domestic airlines existence was not a long-term solution for his people.

"Take the Foreign Service exam," he said. He looked somber; his glowing and magnificent heart did not show.

"But... the competition!" I said.

"I know," Tony answered. "But most of them are assholes."

Backed against a wall in an economic recession with no other good options, as a throwaway I took the FS test.

Who would have known, but I passed it on the first try.

Sandra's Moment (Part One)
January 27, 2015

Nineteen ninety-three. I sat in my cubicle, the window over my back facing the opposite wall without character.

Back in the days of phones, mine rang. It was a friend who was a clerk of a clerk of a clerk of a Supreme Court justice.

"Be here by two," she said. "I'll get you in. It's a case of government employees and their right to publish."

I didn't know much about the subject, but I thought it would be a great opportunity to see Sandra Day O'Connor and Clarence Thomas and the seven others.

As a federal employee, I hadn't gone out pushing the limits on freedom to publish, but I had taken minor risks putting out some tourism articles, and a little book on buying stringed instruments. Nothing classified, and nothing remotely touching U.S. policy in any region.

There's a sense of awe when the justices come out from the red curtain and take their seats on the dais, each creaking and swaying in their individual styles, each in a sacerdotal chair of different size and character, ordered up to fit. I guess one of the privileges is to choose the one you want. Freedom of expression on La-Z-Boy.

I knew I was "witnessing history" when Justice Thomas actually asked a brief question during the proceedings. This has happened only a finite number of times, and never at all since 2006. Thomas-watchers keep track of these rare events, maybe do off-track betting on them.

I don't remember Justice Thomas's question, but I do remember its weak tone, and the disregard of all the others for whatever point he was making. Even he didn't seem really to want an answer.

The issue that day was freedom of expression for federal employees, and in particular an internal rule in the Executive Branch of government that set parameters and limits. For those of us in the Foreign Service, the FAM (Foreign Affairs Manual) was clear-clear-muddled, and read something like this: 1. No classified material, 2. Disclaimer required ("This does not necessarily reflect the opinion of…"), and 3.No text which could adversely affect U.S. foreign policy.

The first two of these were crystal clear and reasonable. The third was a mess waiting to happen. Somebody was racing to finish work on a Friday when that third provision went into the FAM. Like other efforts to govern the future, this lame phrase relied mainly on dumb luck to get the result it wanted.

I'd never been in a Supreme Court Q&A session, and was struck (who wouldn't be?) by the tininess of the little advocates on the floor making their arguments, with the nine indecently massive justices seated above.

And how badly they behave! Ignoring, interrupting, sidetracking, and distracting the advocates as they present their sinuous briefs. Very complicated syllogisms don't get far when they get stopped halfway through. Imagine being down on the humble floor making arguments to ADHD geniuses with absolute authority to cut off and contradict. I think this comes from the European academic tradition of doing unto others as has been done to you unjustly at some point.

The U.S. government (USG) advocate sounded more erudite that day than the other, who was defending an individual. The USG was arguing for limits on publishing content written during off hours by USG officials. The opponent was defending the right of any individual to say anything they wanted, and to publish as well.

After about forty minutes, though, I remember vividly the magisterial moment of Sandra Day O'Connor, who has always been a hero to me.

Never exactly leaving her seat, she seemed to do so, as she leaned over the wide bench on the dais and addressed the microscopic government advocate down on the floor.

Cutting him off in one of his arguments, she said, "You're kidding, right? You're arguing that three million Americans be denied their First Amendment rights? It's a joke, right?"

That pretty much settled it. Arguments were completed and a few weeks later the justices voted (the Founders meant decisions to be presented unanimously in public after internal debate, but voting came in decades later). Something like seven-to-two, the Court found in favor of the individual who had published, and against the Executive Branch of the U.S. government trying to impose restrictions.

So, *ex post facto* and *ipso bipso,* my travel articles had never been "illegal" after all.

A wise friend said to me at the time, "The rule has always been clear: You can say and print anything you want. And we decide when we don't need to keep you on the job any longer."

Sun Tzu in a Cubicle (Part Two)

January 29, 2015

I was trained to manage within rules rather than accepting them unquestioningly. Gravity, for example, doesn't always work in my favor, but I see there isn't much point in trying to defy it. At least without some sort of plan, like Bernoulli's Principle, which keeps airplanes up there. This is above my pay grade.

So when I wrote a book later, in 2003, about U.S. policy in Haiti, the point was not to challenge any system.

It was what André Breton called "automatic writing," only it was based on archival fact instead of subconscious and subliminal spasms. It didn't seem right to me that the UN, OAS, EU, CARICOM, and the governments of seven nations (the "Friends" of Haiti) changed their tune twice a week over a two-year period, then later claimed consistency with regard to the lousy Haitian elections of 2000. They were "good," "bad," "free and fair," "cleverly manipulated," "antidemocratic," and "a sign of political maturation," depending on the whimsy of the day or the wind direction. And the

Haitians, whose opinion never mattered to the international community, took it in the neck.

Just setting the record straight seemed compelling to me. I didn't fixate on the rules any more than I thought to render my work "publishable." At the time, publishing seemed like an Olympic bronze at least.

When it came time to submit my manuscript for "clearance," I looked at the short FAM entry, and realized there was no mention of *where* to submit. And no one seemed to know. I tried Diplomatic Security, who kept the manuscript a few weeks and then sent me a note saying, "Kindly tell us what we are supposed to do with this. And meanwhile come and pick it up at the front door."

Then I tried the Bureau of Western Hemisphere Affairs, which sent back a collegial email, "Good book. What is it we are to do with it?"

I asked a dozen people, but no one knew where "clearance" was supposed to come from.

Finally someone said, "Try Public Affairs," so I did. The FAM said something like, "Failure to respond in 30 days constitutes clearance," but I knew the bureaucracy had other trump cards.

After a few weeks I received an email straight from the Department spokesman's computer: "Do not publish this book." Pretty clear instructions. After so many months trying to get the record straight, and a lot of work getting a narrative out of it, I was peeved.

Pretty naïvely and with genuine innocence, I sent a short email in return: "May I know why not?"

There were some weeks of silence from Public Affairs (PA). I had no idea at the time, but later I learned that PA figured I was pulling a Sun Tzu, and concealing a great power—or feigning one—which could tip them off balance. They tried a Sun Tzu themselves, wanting me and my book just to go away, but never saying so. They gave me the silent treatment for a month, then asked me to come in for a talk.

"Sure," I said. I had no leverage of my own, and got ready to be talked to. I never imagined them wearing conical black hats or the pointy sleeves of the magus. These were my colleagues.

In fact, the meeting took place in the Historian's Office, which is part of Public Affairs, and which had drawn the short straw in being assigned to deal with me and my book. There were six or seven of them on one side of the table, and just me on the other. They weren't smarmy. They just gave me the lookover, guessing I might have some hidden leverage that could possibly outdo them.

We all shook hands, like sumo wrestlers. After a pretty long silence the Historian himself said to me, "Would you be willing at all to discuss some editorial changes to your book?"

"Of course," I said, and I could sense relief from the six or seven on the other side of the table. What was going on here? What author would ever not agree to "discuss" changes? Was I missing something?

The mood became more relaxed. A young official passed me a legal pad with some suggested changes to my manuscript. I looked over the list and quickly saw his changes made no dent at all in the character or direction of the book. One note said, "Our records show that the statement was made April 15, not April 13 as you say," and, "Could you use a word other than 'craven' in paragraph 93?"

In fact, the 100-or-so suggestions actually strengthened my book by increasing its accuracy and by tempering my expressions of disgust with less emotion, rendering them more convincing. This was worth gold to me as a mentorship in historiography. "Do not print this" had morphed into "We will help you make this better. And we won't even charge for the service."

The process took about a year, but resulted in a better book, and finally in a memo from PA to me, "You are now clear to publish."

What the hell was this all about?

The junior Historian whose desk my book had landed on took me to lunch after it was all over, the whole jujitsu and kabuki and karaoke I never understood: "It's a fine book. We all liked it. We were just afraid you might have a lawyer or something, and we imagined—God forbid—another trip over to the Supreme Court."

"Lawyer?!" I said. "Who can afford these things?"

"Well, we didn't know for sure. So now they're trying to rewrite the FAM to make things clearer. But the clearer they get, the more they stray into First Amendment rights. So to hell with it. If you're free this Saturday, come over and meet the wife and kids."

"Gladly," I said.

The result was *A Haiti Chronicle*, published about a year later than it might have been, to have any currency of timeliness. But anyway it's all now on the record.

Be one of the few ever to read it—it's ISBN 9781412033992. And, as they say, thank you for your time.

Not Funny Any More
March 14, 2015

During a recent snowstorm, I went into the recesses of the house that don't get much attention most of the time, and found old books I hadn't seen in a few decades.

I rediscovered Walt Kelly, a great American and creator of *Pogo*, a loosely political, syndicated cartoon depicting friendly and not-so-friendly creatures from Florida's Okefenokee Swamp. Anyone who was a teenager in America in the 1950s or 1960s remembers *Pogo*; others might not.

The protagonist, an opossum, served as avatar for the author, observing and innocently questioning the neighbors around him. Pogo stood on the shoulders of Archy, the philosophical and reflective cockroach (enamored of a cat) created by the magisterial Don Marquis, from yet an earlier age. Aesop and LaFontaine were the classical masters of the genre of anthropomorphized animals created for ethical and moral examples (good and bad) for humans to go by. The form allows the author to avert ad hominem assaults, and has been used traditionally to keep authors out of trouble in times of oppression. The *roman à clef*, the political cartoon's literary equivalent, makes topical references while setting up plausible deniability.

Walt Kelly's humanized caricatures included a mole in denial ("blindness"), a muskrat speaking in Gothic letters ("hypocrite" and "bully"), a female skunk with French accent ("sexy"), a cigar-smoking alligator ("benign-if-reckless"), an owl ("wisdom, sort of"), a pair of crows ("observers/Greek chorus") and other creatures which helped the reader single out contemporaneous individuals seeking to find order in a world threatened by communism, nuclear holocaust, social reorganizations of the most bizarre types, and a moral pathway to decency.

As I went through these archaeological treasures that snowy day, I came upon Walt Kelly's equivalent of Mark Twain's *King Leopold's Soliloquy*, Twain's *cri de coeur* when he found out about cruelty and genocide in the Belgian Congo in the late nineteenth century. All masterpieces have antecedents.

The Jack Acid Society Black Book, written and published shortly after Senator Joe McCarthy's political demise in 1953, is Kelly's spoof of the John Birch Society (JBS), which guided the political right in America but was never taken too seriously in many quarters. JBS, still active today with a glitzy website, was created by Robert Welch in the late 1950s to combat communist ideology and limit the authorities of the U.S. government. Today he would be a Tea Party advocate. JBS was opposed to world government ("collectivism"), the civil rights movement and legislation of the 1960s which it explicitly linked to communist fifth column actions, and wealth redistribution. It endorsed Christian values as a guide to political and ethical actions.

McCarthyism did not deploy firing squads, but it was, well, creepy. Because its ideology was so odd and did not conduct massive killings, it was considered a fringe group at the time. The nation was mainly relieved when McCarthy himself ("Have you no shame?") was undone by Senate investigation in 1953. The persecutorial spirit lived on, though, and morphed into bizarre political groups which were mainly mocked at the time, but have since gotten their hands on huge funding sources.

Hear Walt Kelly from 1957, in his tongue-in-cheek introduction to *The Jack Acid Society Black Book*:

> All of the right-wing societies which might be confused with the Jack Acid Society are understandably as nervous as a troop of elephants trying to talk on water. They claim to be apprehensive of the far left, the left and even the middle, but they also keep a sharp eye on each other.

Kelly had masterful wit and a critical eye, but lived his most creative period when it seemed that malignant McCarythism had been fought back into its cage and growling orneriness. These were halcyon days when the genie was thought to be back in the bottle. Ridiculing hypocrites counted as good, clean fun:

> There has also been a little God snatching and flag appropriating here and there. Most societies claim that God is on their side, and by implication, it is questionable whether He is on any other side. However, the Jack Acids were formed first, and first come is first served. If the flag and God belong to anyone, they belong to them.

My point here is that these discredited foolishnesses seem to have metastasized in 2015 America, and become a serious business. They raise serious money and malign innocent actors in the civil society.

Kelly's incarnation of the religious right, the prattling Molester Mole, says, "We are on God's side and all who oppose us are against God! ...It is not the enemy with the bomb who is the most dangerous... it is the traitor in our midst..."

I need not connect the dots to recent statements and actions from our malignant Right; the reader is able to do so. What seemed to be risible ravings in the 1950s have now become formidable political forces with powerful backers. Their intent seems to be to replace decency and established international norms which have minimized conflict over five centuries. New words and deeds, now emboldened and fully funded, unravel our precarious world for yet undefined objectives. It will not be pleasing if they succeed in doing so.

This Happened March 20, and It Could Happen to You

March 23, 2015

Land line rings at 3:00 p.m. Usually I'm out at that hour, but I happen to be on a brief pass-through at my house, and I take the call on the fourth ring.

"The Internal Revenue Service is filing a lawsuit against you for non-payment of $6,000 in taxes. You must call the following number..."

Sounds like a scam, but I call the number out of "excess of caution," and I get through on the third try.

"We will seize your bank account, remove your social security number and driver's license."

The line goes dead. It's the sort of experience which seems 98 percent phony, more like 99—but one wants to follow through. I redial the number.

"You are Dan Whitman, right?" they say. They've got my name and unlisted home number. Fair enough.

"There is a big problem with your tax payments."

"You say you are the Internal Revenue Service?" I ask.

"Yes, calling from New Jersey."

"I'm not saying I'll do anything for you, but can you tell me what you want from me?"

"You must fill out a Moneygram for $642 dollars and call this number again, and we will direct you on the next step."

I say, "Great, down from $6,000 to $642. You bring me good news. But if you're a scam, you're still not telling your victims what you want them to do. Do you really make money this way? And by the way, how are things in India these days?"

"Do you know who is Narenda Modi?" the voice says.

[In case you think I am making any of this up, I ask you to believe I would put my hand on the flame to assure you this all happened.]

"I think he is the prime minister of India."

"And what is your opinion of him?"

"I can have no opinion, I have never been to India. Long live globalization."

The voice at the other end softens a bit. "In fact I am calling you from Pakistan, not New Jersey."

"Pardon me for stereotyping; I sensed a time difference between us."

"It is 2:00 a.m. here."

"Well then, now that we have settled what is happening, maybe you could tell me what it was you wanted from me? Not that I have any plans to do anything for you. Was it my credit card number you wanted?"

"We don't want your fucking credit card number."

I count to three. "I guess when you say 'fucking,' it is likely you do not represent the Internal Revenue Service. It's not their style."

"That is correct; this is a scam. From Pakistan."

"Well now, that's interesting. You sound like a nice young man and I'm sorry you have to work with a criminal organization. But how do you expect to get any money from your victims, though, if you don't even tell them what it is you want them to do for you?"

"I hate this job. I have student debt to pay."

"I'm really sorry. My name is Dan, as you pointed out. If there is anything about your circumstances you think I can help with, let me know."

"I have never cheated a person. I want you to know this is a scam. This is my last day on this fucking job, and I can't wait to leave."

"Sorry."

"Call this number again after we hang up, and one of my colleagues will tell you what you are supposed to do, Moneygram and all the rest. But don't follow any of the instructions. Tell them you are very concerned and worried, and want to pay your debts."

"If it helps you, I will do so, otherwise I think I won't bother."

"That's entirely up to you. I am in a difficult situation."

"I realize. And I am sorry. No one seems to have what they need anymore. There is lots of money in the world, but I don't know where it is. Normal people don't usually get much of it."

"You are right. It has been a pleasure to talk to you. God bless."

"God bless you too, and goodbye."

I am not sure what the lesson to learn is here. Perhaps, criminals are frightened little puppies like the rest of us. Perhaps, distrust everyone at all times. Perhaps, get more information through cordial dealings. Perhaps, Pakistan is over the brink, and its good people are more desperate than we thought. My only advice would be, talk things through, keep calm, and never make a false move. Some scams will work better than others, and our current state of confusion and high tech indicates more vigilance. In the forest, each predator gets one turn, and our job as victims is to make the predators starve. Not a bright vision of the future, but it can be a little bright if we carry on and keep the dialogue going.

Faulkner Trending

March 23, 2015

There's a note trending now among forty former practitioners of public diplomacy, each one narrating zany experiences in the field from the glory days from when the United States "did" culture overseas. Louis Armstrong, Dave Brubeck, and others went at great personal and financial sacrifice to serve their country by charming publics in hostile nations and freeing the human spirit in ways that transcended political differences. They were great heroes, yet to be replaced as we seek to tweet ourselves out of the Islamic State and Putinism. Long may our efforts live, and all power to the tweet if that is what strikes people's consciousness, really.

We know that William Faulkner used to chart out his drinking binges on the calendar. Faulkner was America's Proust. His Nobel Prize acceptance speech in 1950 was possible only through the connivance of his family, who X'd out dates on the calendar and deceived him to think it was a week later than it really was. This is good urban myth, but I take it as true. December 10 he gave one of the most memorable of all Nobel speeches, speaking of "the ding-dong of doom" in an age of nuclear proliferation bringing humans to the brink of annihilation.

Public diplomacy colleagues are now coming forward with their good anecdotes of trying to keep Faulkner sober just for certain occasions while he traveled overseas for the U.S. government, spreading goodwill through his transcendent prose and supernational consciousness.

Others have been sending in their responding anecdotes on managing cultural exchange over challenges of ego, logistics, circumstances, and stories that can now be told decades after they took place. Pianos being hauled up steep cliffs by pulley, dancers falling off stages to protest against creaky floorboards.

Here is my humble contribution: Mark O'Connor, virtuoso country fiddler and mandolin player, went to the Middle East in 1983, sent by something called Arts America, a division of the U.S. Information Agency. Arts America was snuffed out in its sleep by President Clinton's USIA Administrator, Joe Duffey, in the mid-1990s as a cost-saving measure.

I was O'Connor's "roadie," setting up venues for him in Syria, Jordan, and Egypt through coordination with cultural attachés at U.S. Embassies in those countries. I provided bananas during intermissions for potassium restoration, and was presented a small medallion of pewter bananas in appreciation at the end of the trip. O'Connor and his brilliant ensemble performed in Palmyra and Aleppo in now-devastated Syria, and also in Amman, Cairo, and a few other venues.

In the salad days of U.S. culture overseas, we also went to Alexandria, Egypt, where I'm told there was once a library of importance. We toured the atmospheric city, then checked in with the U.S. Branch Public Affairs Officer, who will go unnamed in this article. Mr. X briefed us about security concerns in the friendly city (pro forma, since Americans were most welcome at that time). Then he sat us down and explained some opaque issue about booking discrepancies in the city's opera house, built in 1918 and opened in 1921, French style since the French had passed briefly through Egypt some decades earlier.

The performing group—Mark and five others—took in this information and proceeded with the stage plans and adaptations to the venue of the day.

That evening in June, we set up the stage for country and bluegrass music, which O'Connor and his group performed magisterially. The building was dilapidated, and my task was to hold a spotlight from an upper balcony, since the apparatus was deteriorating and kept falling like the head of a dozing narcoleptic. The spotlight was needed in order for anything to be visible on the stage for the thousand or so spectators who were slowly filling the hall. It kicked up a lot of dust and at one point seemed to ignite a fire in the hall, though the heat and dust turned out not to be lethal. "The band is hot tonight!" one of the performers said appropriately into the mic, knowing the audience would not quite get the import of his word play.

Curiously, people came in late, and late seating was arranged for a few hundred people. The audience seemed interested in the performance, but there was a distraction in the hall. We of the O'Connor group noted an odd disorder but had no way of judging what it came from or what it meant.

At intermission, the U.S. Alexandria Branch Post Public Affairs Officer came to us and said he was needed at his residence, something about babysitting for his three children. He excused himself and left. We never quite got the cue from his earlier mention of "booking confusion," and never caught on that this was a serious matter. WTF.

Large crowds scuffled outside the opera house, and police were beating them back with sticks and non-lethal whips. Backstage, Egyptians in exotic garb were silently forming ordered rows, their presence unexplained. They were dressed in Pharaonic textiles with feathers and fancy hats, preening themselves for some performance we knew nothing about.

People continued filing in to the hall even during the intermission of the O'Connor performance, and we were getting dirty looks both from the hall and from backstage.

Putting two and two together, I realized the "booking confusion" was in fact a double booking in the opera house, one by the O'Connor group and the other for the Egyptian national folklore dance troupe, booked at the same time that evening. The U.S. Alexandria Branch Post Public Affairs Officer must have known this, but left us hanging, with crowds fighting with police outside, the Egyptian national dance troupe in disarray about their stage being preempted by an American music group no one wanted to hear, and spotlights in a hall that seemed to be on fire.

I suggested that we finish up the performance very quickly and allow the others on the stage. We did this to polite applause and vamoosed to our hotel where the musicians ate bananas and drank beer.

This was not an ideal cultural presentation, and did not much good for America's image abroad. But the music was great. When we returned to Washington I reported the incident to central planners in Arts America, but I think they did not believe such a thing could happen. Thirty-five years later, it is time to get this story on the record. And somewhere, a former Branch Public Affairs Officer gets a nice pension and fertilizes a lawn, though on the latter I am only guessing.

Small Enough to Succeed

May 15, 2015

May 28, one of these candidates will succeed Donald Kaberuka as African Development Bank (AfDB) president. Kaberuka's ten-year run got the African Development Bank up to $3.16 billion in loans and grants per annum to infrastructure projects on the continent, pretty modest compared to the World Bank's $15 billion. China puts in about the same $15 billion per annum in investments, which some would consider "real money."

With Africa's visible problems, it nevertheless churns on at six per cent growth as a whole, positioning it to move up the world scale in the near future as China's growth slows. Africa has the natural resources China doesn't; if the OECD, World Bank, and U.S. government really mean it in combating corruption in developing countries, the Dark Continent's future will turn bright. Optimism on any topic will appear to be naïve until the day it comes to fruition, then predictors get the last laugh.

The AfDB (unfortunately "BAD" in French) is one of the most agile capital pools going. April 16, seven of the eight candidates came to present themselves at Washington's most development-friendly think tank, the Center for Global Development (CGD). CGD's moderator Rajesh Mirchandani led a lively discussion, bringing out the best in each candidate. See the video here:

http://www.cgdev.org/event/who-will-lead-african-development-bank

The discussion was not so much a debate as a revelation. Any of the CGD seven could win an intellectual "beauty contest" – more importantly, all incarnated what one wants most in a banker: boring predictability. I mean this in the most positive and admiring way. Mirchandani reminded the audience that we were present not to "vote" but to listen to the candidates for the job. The AfDB will be in excellent hands, regardless of the outcome – anybody out there disagree?

The world GNP—estimated by "big data" to be $75.62 trillion—dwarfs all development capital funds, but the latter can be crucial pivots to bring benefits for rich, poor, labor markets, manufacturing and services. In French, it's called *"engrainer"* – carrying along with micro pulses, sand in the oyster. Development matters and can succeed, if the CGD agenda has credibility. Lots of data and anecdotal evidence back them up.

The themes at the CGD discussion were predictable and consistent: infrastructure, capacity, private sector, transparency, accountability, natural resource management, renewable energy, consolidation, innovation, regional integration, results. None of these goals will be easily achieved, all will be key in advancing Africa's future. As candidate Duarte said (I paraphrase), "China? Patagonia? No big difference: the mercantilists did the same." This frankness and pragmatic acknowledgment, shared by all seven candidates present, augur well for the AfDB.

Huge challenges remain: climate change, corruption reduction, visible and measureable results which would bring in more capital, regional integration on a continent with ridiculous national borders and self-harming tariffs, natural resource management in a field of past and present plunder. But Africa and its resources are vast, and even waste has not dented its potential. Imagine, an African middle class able to purchase things. And there is China (as we others could be) to provide the demand they can now pay for.

Would I vote for Sidibe, Adesina, Duarte, Kamara, Sakala, Ayed, Bedoumra , Ahmed? I say any one will do. Mali, Nigeria, Cape Verde, Sierra Leone, Zimbabwe, Tunisia, Chad, Ethiopia: someone saw to it that small countries were represented with the large, Francophone with Anglophone with Lusophone, stilted versus flourishing markets. All are encouraged in a new collaborative openness. We may not see "The United States of Africa" anytime soon, but borders notwithstanding, a collaborative spirit seems to emerge on the Continent. Some of the candidates put out glossy brochures, like Kordjé Bedoumbra's "Mes ambitions pour la BAD," or Akinwumi Adesina's "Building on the successes of the African Development Bank and positioning to effectively address emerging challenges" (yawn).

The point is, there is well-focused passion in all these candidates, and one will take over. Got extra capital to spare? Put it into the continent where even the plunderers never managed to stifle its potential. No extra capital, like most of us? Look, anyway, to the AfDB's modest past and future investments. Something could happen here: all boats could yet rise, though impediments could tighten their grip as well. The suspense merits some close attention, with optimism the paradigm that can best bring the outcome benefiting all.

Looking Before You Leap
May 16, 2015

At $50.3 billion (FY '16 projected), the U.S. budget for diplomacy and overseas development is a pretty good deal. One-tenth the spending of the Department of Defense and well below two per cent of national public expenditures, it comes in almost unnoticeable to people like me, baffled by zeroes.

Even so, it's real money and needs to stand up to scrutiny.

When Secretary of State Hillary Clinton saw the Pentagon's Quadrennial Defense Review, she said, "I want one of those." Thus, the Quadrennial Diplomaty and Development Review (QDDR), launched in 2011 by an exceedingly smart public servant, Anne-Marie Slaughter.

Now, four years later, sure enough, there's a new version, and just about on time. The QDDR is not (yet) a Congressional mandate, but maybe ought to be, and could become a requirement so the CBO can see what it gets for the taxpayers' money.

Rolled out April 28, the Kerry QDDR took the bureaucratic-sounding title, "Enduring Leadership in a Dynamic World."

News for you: Hillary Clinton's "Three Ds" (Defense, Diplomacy, Development) have been replaced, and are now Data, Diagnostics, Design. I would say "intelligent design," but let's not get into that.

Newness is so commonplace these days (and will be from now on) that it hardly is new. Caution, more than modesty, leads QDDR Special Representative Tom Perriello to promise that his worthy product has built-in obsolescence.

At one of the various rollouts, this one May 14 at the Brookings Institution, panelists talked about big data as the new transparency. Increasingly, it is seen at least in the public sector as a public holding. Indeed, "knowledge is power" has a stale ring to it, as if my knowledge were your disadvantage. I've always thought that knowledge shared is knowledge increased (don't hoard it!). This seems to be behind the buzzword "knowledge sharing;" I think I even heard the acronym "KS" at the Brookings session.

The Brookings discussion was subtitled "Using Data to Exercise Smart Power," and so the Clinton legacy remains, eschewing "soft power" altogether. Once I had a chance to ask Joe Nye what he thought about the elimination, entirely, of one of his three entities. Jovially, he answered, "Smart power is big enough to include both smart and soft. Plus, no American politician could survive using a word like 'soft.'" (Hard power, the really expensive stuff, is what you use when all else fails, and hasn't had a good run in recent decades.)

With the new QDDR, method becomes strategy. Undergraduates, listen up: data is the basis of social improvement, because it must be "understandable, actionable, and compelling." If you can get a handle on this, your future may be bright. The New Religion is not belief, but application.

Importantly, Brookings's masterful George Ingram included enlightened number crunchers from State, AID, the Millennium Challenge Corporation (MCC), and the private sector on his panel.

All leaned in, all drew on the tics and peculiarities of the others' approaches to data. There seemed a consensus that, like air, data should be a shared entity. Private and public together. In development, for example, the donor tradition of "getting your own" may be going extinct. Anyone's data is fair game, if it's "verifiable."

The example all liked was the use of cell phone tracking to indicate who was where when. I don't mean for forensic purposes. But actual use of roads and other infrastructure can debunk a lot of developmental theory if the latter is fanciful.

I don't know much from data. Nor can I present it to others pictorially to save my life. But I think it's like gravity: defy it at your peril. There's a closer link than ever between research, science, and policy. This is good, since policy by instinct has never served well. Policy, too, has a moral and ethical aspect more embedded than before. As religious beliefs decline sharply in the United States according to recent studies, behavior that helps and does not harm others fills the void. Even the Pope says, "Atheists who do good are redeemed." Or more exactly, "We must meet one another doing good. 'But I don't believe, Father; I am an atheist!' But do good: we will meet one another there [in Heaven]."

Are we so far from big data here? Not really. Descartes, who banished subjectivity from what he allowed himself to "believe," would have taken data as something you could hang on to. If "data" equals "belief" in the New Religion, then "monitoring and evaluation" becomes "proof." For those who need it, that is.

If it sounds as if I understand any of this, I'm bluffing. I don't get it, but I see what's happening among those who run the world at this brief moment. They all say, "We will soon be superseded," but that may be a coy bit of plausible deniability. Empirical data—showing facts over "values"—seems to be the new helio- or geocentric world. Groove to it, and check out the 2015 QDDR. It's not as fun as religion and the music is definitely less moving, but maybe if it grows from the ground up, it might turn into something.

Bronx Cheer for a Danish Court

June 8, 2015

In a world of metastasizing injustices, Denmark would be one of the last places to get a red flag for public policy abuse.

Still, the Danish Supreme Court stepped in it June 3 in a case against Bent Jensen, who conveyed declassified records into a publication in 2007. The outcome has Danish writers and publishers running for cover.

The plot is hardly *Hamlet*. Jensen, a Danish historian, was preparing his 2000-page history on the Cold War, and was given access to declassified Danish intelligence files. He cited several indicating that journalist Jørgen Dragsdahl ("Drowse-dehl") was a KGB agent in the 1980s. Many had thought so. This was the opinion of intelligence operatives, including the second-in-command of the Police Intelligence unit (PET), not an "official" government position. Anyway, no one goes to the gibbet in Denmark.

Dragsdahl wrote for *Information*, a left-of-center daily with modest circulation, but which made the rounds among Danish university and high school teachers. In a Cold War gambit, he published a daily article in the upper lefthand corner of his paper (upper left is the prime spot in Danish journalism) throwing brickbats at NATO for maintaining a defensive radar station in Thule, at the northernmost point of Greenland. Nothing wrong with defense, you might say. But this was part of the protocol in the 1972 Anti-Ballistic Missile Treaty (ABM) between the United States and Soviet Union. ABM limited the placement and number of radars the two superpowers could have, on the assumption that a weak defense meant less risk of offense. It's part of what saved the world from annihilation in the 1970s and '80s.

The banned technology was something called "phased-array radar," which was... well, find an expert to explain that one. The United States said the USSR had one illegally in Krasnoyarsk (2,094 miles from Moscow); the Soviets said we had one illegally in Thule, northern Greenland (2,616 miles from Washington, DC). The point of ABM was to remove certain defenses from Moscow and Washington, so no one would pull a Doctor Strangelove. People like the admirable General Brent Scowcroft understood the technology of these machines, but not many others did.

Back to Dragsdahl. In the Cold War, the two sides luckily put out more rhetoric and public argument than nuclear exchanges. Hence the talkers carried a lot of weight. Never mind the proxy wars in Africa, Latin America, and Asia—that was a different department.

Writing for a key audience in Denmark, Dragsdahl took up the Thule issue like a dog with a bone. *Information* even created a logo for his daily column in 1986 and into 1987, which made the series seem more of a campaign than a sample of investigative journalism. It went on for months, and seemed a little fishy at the time. More interesting journalism might have taken up the relative merits and demerits of the Thule and Krasnoyarsk radars (well, and also one called Fylingdales, in the UK). Thule was never an issue until the U.S. poked at Krasnoyarsk. When it did, the USSR opened up its info machine with both barrels. Since Thule was in Greenland under Danish sovereignty, the target came up clear in the Soviet crosshairs. The *Information* coverage was more than a little one-sided, and solidly pro-Soviet. We now know that Soviet propaganda was targeting especially the "weak links" of NATO: Netherlands and

Denmark. Understandably, an agile KGB jousted at possible tipping points to see if they could make them tip. Anyone with their hand of cards might have done the same.

[Danish intelligence services never found a direct link to the Thule story, but did in a forgery case of American field manual material, concocted by KGB creative writers and published in translation by Dragsdahl in *Information* in 1979.] In 1986-87, Dragsdahl seemed either a bit obsessed, or possibly in someone's pocket. Bent Jensen says he found material in declassified Danish police records stating that, after three years of phone taps, the Danish intelligence decided Dragsdahl was working for the benefit of the USSR, with a specific connection to the KGB (money? No hard facts on that, though a 2013 court document shows Danish intelligence vouching for various Dragsdahl-KBG meetings, including one in Vienna, March 20, 1986, and citing him as an "exceptionally useful agent of influence). No one ever claimed these were illegal acts in Denmark at the time, and Danish police never considered an indictment (imagine how this would have gone down in the United States). I'm not saying American paranoia was a more or less effective way of fighting a cold war than Danish permissiveness. It's Bent Jensen I feel for.

By 2013 the affair seemed over, as the former chief of Danish intelligence Ole Stig Andersen testified in Jensen's favor and said Jensen's case was solid. Dragsdahl averred he had "contacts" with the KGB, but only to seek help for getting his Russian girlfriend out of the USSR. The case went on for some years, going against Jensen in 2010 and with him in 2013. Then, last week, the Supreme Court reversed previous findings and slammed Jensen with a 10,000 kroner fine (about $1500 U.S.). In its five-to-two decision, it also made Jensen pay for Dragsdahl's legal fees and court costs, the whole thing totaling 685,000 DKK, or about $102,000. Not much of a tort case by U.S. standards, but a big deal in Denmark.

The charges (*"injurie"* in Danish) are something between a criminal and civil offense in the United States. Dragsdahl nailed Jensen for something like defamation and came out smiling, and waving a Soviet-period flag.

In a passionate and defensive editorial June 5, *Information* called out centrist and right-of-center dailies *Berlingske Tidende* and *Jyllands-Posten* for committing "disinformation" in saying that Jensen had found his material in unclassified police documents. The previous day, *Jyllands-Posten* had written in its own editorial, "Bent Jensen never called Jørgen Dragsdahl an agent himself, but only cited compromising documents from the KGB and PET [the Danish equivalent]."

Information did some digging, and found the quote they wanted, from January 14, 2007. The more conservative paper had run a headline, "'The archives show he was a KGB agent,' concludes the professor." Meaning, he didn't just quote a police file, he actually *drew a conclusion*. Heavens! Now he's a criminal.

The proverb goes, "Small town, big problems." Vengeance is still dear in small, well-organized countries. Money amounts are relative, but honor isn't. The Danish blogosphere this week shows everyone has a strong opinion, one way or the other.

Thanks anyway, Jørgen and others, for the geography lessons on northern Greenland. Waiting for your series on the area 2,094 miles east of Moscow, which I understand has flowers or permafrost, depending on the month. And no, I'm not starting up a GoFundMe for the venerable Bent Jensen, but I hope someone does.

Saved by a Tux
June 15, 2015

"Négritude," fashionable in the first half of the twentieth century, was a precursor of Black Pride for francophone countries. It was a play on a French word which wasn't flattering, though a little less abusive than the English equivalent. It flew in the face of colonial condescension.

Because it had an element of assimilationism, it was rebuked by later generations, but put out some fine poetry while the going was good.

Of the founders—Aimé Césaire (Martinique), Léon Damas (French Guiana), and Léopold Sédar Senghor (Senegal)—the latter two were actually members of the French National Assembly, as France's earlier reach conferred special status more on some colonial subjects than others. Wherever the French flag flew came the *"mission civilisatrice"* which stooped to embrace its people and make them into little Frenchmen. Though négritude ridiculed that idea, it didn't ridicule it enough to gain permanent respect or status. It was a good try at the time.

Later generations didn't realize what these guys were up against: French colonialism was not all that benign, and after all lasted to the 1960s and beyond. By hearsay anyway, local administrators cracked men's heads like walnuts between planks of wood, connected by a pivot, for not paying taxes or agricultural tribute. A Malian once told me he had seen this as a boy as recently as the 1940s.

Francophone African ferment came partly from French schools, where classmates read Arthur de Gobineau's treatise, *Essai sur l'inégalité des races humaines,* and its pseudoscientific explanations for the inferiority of darker-skinned people. This, even as the French were taking on the task of drilling into them archaic verb forms like the imperfect subjunctive (which they did very well). There was cognitive dissonance here, and some intellectuals had to come and set it straight.

Négritude founders Césaire, Damas, and Senghor were close personal friends and got together when circumstances permitted.

In some of his later years, Léon Damas lived in suburban Maryland, where I met him a couple of times in the 1970s. He was a great poet, also a satirist, mimicker, and trouble-maker. He hated pomp and took every opportunity to ridicule it.

He told me this story one hot summer evening:

"A few years back I was visiting Dakar and decided to call up my friend Senghor. He said, 'Come over tonight, I'm having a reception for some key contacts.'

"I said, 'Léo, you know I'm not into these sorts of things; I like to just have a light meal and go to bed.'

"Senghor said I had to come, that friendship depended on it. What to do? I realized these things are formal—I mean, really formal—and I'd need a tux. Where, where to find a tux? So I found a formal wear shop and rented a smoking jacket just for the evening.

"I got to the president's house and felt so out of place. Everyone there was dressed to the nines, knew what wine to take with what *amuse-gueule*, and I just didn't know where to put myself. I tried to disappear into a corner, but Senghor pulled me out and put me in front of everyone. The place was packed with parliamentarians, ministers, journalists, military brass. What to do? I went up to the one with fanciest uniform, this one even had epaulettes. Epaulettes, you realize. [He flicked his own shoulders to stress the point.]

"I didn't know what to do or say, so I went up to the one with the fanciest uniform and said, 'So, when's the coup?' [*'Alors, c'est pour quand, le coup d'état?'*]

"Well, how was I supposed to know he actually *was* planning a coup? He thought somehow I'd figured this out and had unmasked him! Wanting at least not to be executed, he figured his best chance was to go over to President Senghor on the spot. He did, and confessed, and the coup was foiled."

I'll never know if the story was entirely true, but—hand on fire—I vow that Damas told it as above. A tux and some jet lag saved Senegalese democracy, at least that evening.

True or not, some stories are too good not to tell.

Not Taking Sides Yet
July 1, 2015

I'm just back from a week south of the border with 12,000 of my closest friends. Information and computer technology (ICT) was the subject of discussion, and may yet democratize the world if anything can. I'm not a real teacher, but gave it a shot some decades ago in high school, and again in recent times at the university level. I use the Internet all the time, consider it a blessing. I receive many messages each day showing methodologies and techniques which can meet the challenges and impositions of the digital age.

Latin America is full of brilliant and dedicated people, and as a continent it benefits from having a lingua franca (well, two or three) and no state-to-state conflicts. We should take closer note of how they carry on, the complete ease in conversing across borders, the many friendly rivalries which seem to benefit all.

Governments which can afford it are getting tablets and laptops out into their hinterlands, with a dizzying array of apps which shorten and simplify elementary and secondary education, as well as lower the wall between employers' needs and students' abilities and training. This could bring a leap in productivity and, very importantly, match young graduates with jobs and bring down unemployment.

Nothing ominous here, and I'm all for it.

Here is my issue: what we used to call the Digital Divide (it still exists of course) is morphing into an evangelism. Its very friendly and open-minded advocates appear to have the rest of us in one of two categories, but none other: likeminded members or likely converts. I'm very willing to go to as far as the "credo" in the New Religion, but it doesn't seem to satisfy the proselytes. They are compassionate with generationally-challenged individuals such as myself, but in their breaking of idols they lightly damage the walls and pillars that keep the whole structure up. I think this will come out fine in the end.

To explain: I enter a huge hall with private booths welcoming visitors to admire and maybe purchase the new technologies. A lot of it looks like bells and whistles, and takes us from the "liberal education" we used to value, now put to the admittedly noble service of easing the job search for youngsters who seek and deserve it. The inventors, conducting sophisticated research on today's children's shrinking attention span, adapt their product to the consumer rather than what we used to do in requiring concentration for as long as it took to learn something. Little fingers now eagerly touch simulations of things (colors, numbers, animals, shapes…) instead of anything which exists in the natural world. We call them "icons." Actually they are holographs recreated to show what the iconoclasts meant to leave behind. I love iconoclasts even if I'm not one myself, and surely our educational system costing up to one hundred grand a year at the tertiary level cannot and should not last much longer, so this is a great alternative.

But listen up: the iconoclasts have broken up the school room (yes, it's obsolete, I guess) and they do this curious, circular thing of addressing each pupil singly through handheld devices, thus fragmenting the process to individualize the experience. Then they introduce their new technologies and apps to bring the pupils together somehow at a later point in the learning process. Each student works at her own pace and level in figuring out how angles work in triangles and parallelograms, but then must come together later to reach the real conclusions under a teacher's guidance.

Seems a bit roundabout to me.

The believers can easily prove that this improves test scores, and I am glad of it. I am imagining those few who may learn better off the screen than on, and where they may end up once they are cordoned off as digital illiterates.

Increasingly these applications replace words with images, and I think I see where that will take us if anyone ever has to write a cogent paragraph at some time in the future. Or maybe the paragraph will go the way of moveable type, but I am coming up short in seeing how Faulkner or Flaubert will fare as pictograms.

I'm all for icons, maybe less so for the "clasts." The haste in sweeping away prior gadgets (books, for example, which are now forbidden in some university courses in the U.S.) could leave us with a brilliant future and not much of a past. Survival for nine billion people in climate change may indeed require putting the past on "pause," but I don't see how this really democratizes knowledge, the stated goal of the new technologies.

At one of the five hundred (sic!) seminars during the week of June 21-26, I was outed publicly as "an academic." This was done in a friendly and teasing way, and I know it was meant affectionately. But it neutralized my comments. I had a pretty ingenuous question about how products offered online for free can make enough profit to keep their fine developments going. I think because of the Scarlet Letter A ("Academic") on my forehead, the answer had nothing much to do with the question, but, rather, a warmhearted effort to get a rare resister into the fold and onto the wagon.

I'm not a resister. I even said so, twice, but no one believed me. The discussion kept circling back to the credo ("new technologies are wonderful") and I had already reached that point long before.

I don't think I will be euthanized just yet; these are very friendly people. I might even be welcomed eventually into a world I find a little creepy and authoritarian. I think I may be accepted by some as a harmless contrarian, but it would be for the wrong reasons. I do not hug the hard-copy books or value rote memorization of dates, texts, tables of elements. I am not nostalgic for the wooden blocks that taught me colors and shapes. I even spend a lot of time at the screen, mostly with text and news, less with apps. So far I am entitled to use and love the technologies in my own way, easing the tasks I care about, and ignoring the others.

I look forward, only, to shedding the epidermis of evangelism ("This really is great." Yes, I get it) and finding the skin of substance beneath. Merely admiring and respecting changes to speed up democracy and equitable distribution of information (I do) doesn't seem to be enough. I must be dazzled (I'm not) and have to repeat the credo until someone thinks I really mean it.

Today's gentle Lutheranism little resembles the inflammatory zeal of its first appearance in Europe's murderous history. If change is happening today faster than we can even say "change," then I look forward to a speedy maturation of the new New Religion so any of us can be given a pass for taking from it what we want, and leaving the rest.

I know for sure that if I were a fifth grader today, learning mainly through the screen would turn me into a dropout. This is not nostalgia or resistance or generational obtuseness, it just is.

More humans than ever will advance for the benefit of all, in the wireless world of apps. This is good. Credo that. Some, though, will drift to the charms of their own imagination, or tales told from one mouth to another's ear, lost in a vocabulary of the apps they may never learn. They will be digital dropouts. These too are humans, and there may be more of them than some think.

My Three Weapons
July 31, 2015

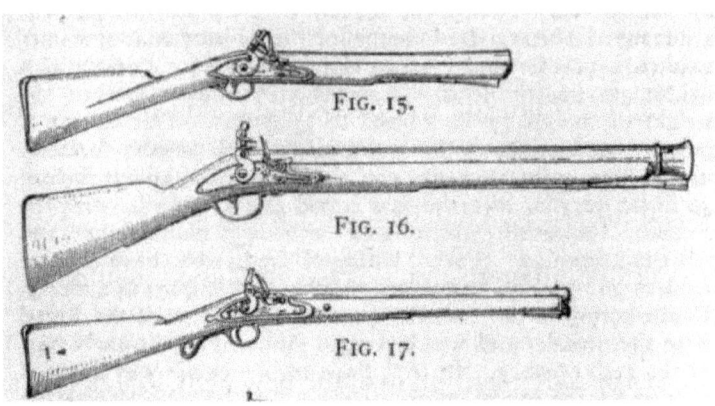

It went like this: a smile, a business card, and a camera. With these three WMDs we faced down an armed police squad and ran them off a property they had invaded.

Yaoundé, 2006. Jim (not his real name) had picked Cameroon off the internet and came on a one-way trip to perform a religious mission.

He was not on good terms with his church, but took Jesus as a role model and I think he believed in God, though we never really discussed it. He stepped way over his head into the sometimes sinister world of good works, where predators stalk to extort imported moneys from well-meaning, gullible donors in the United States.

He signed on to an orphanage run by a phony local nun. Soon enough he found the children were being beaten and abused, while the nun pocketed the funds coming from the U.S.-based church. Sister Margaret (not her real name, either) had teeth and local contracts and plenty of vitriol to keep her precarious perch just above the bottom of the social ladder. Honor, money, grazing rights, and social standing were all mixed into a bulwark against penury, and she would intimidate, bribe, blackmail, kill, to maintain them. Who wouldn't, when the abyss was a step away?

Altruistically but recklessly, Jim got the battered orphans out of Sister Margaret's little prison, and even managed to work up a file with notarized statements from the children's relatives (uncles, siblings, AIDS-stricken mothers…) handing guardians' rights over to him.

The problem was, Jim was a foreigner, and xenophobes had figured out how to use "trafficking in children" against those who would remove children from local custody, taking food money with them. It was to be a fight to the finish. Jim had some resources and the ability to keep a legal paper trail. But Sister Margaret had local toughs and enough bribe money to get some police and "social workers" on her side. She wasn't about to give those up. Nor was compromise an option in the zero-sum game.

The local police gave twenty-four hours' notice before invading the children's house, to put them in the street with nowhere to go. This may seem heartless, perhaps no more so than any imperfect legal system where rules come before empathy to assure a social order in a wider context. I'm not being relativistic here, just trying to imagine what would be on the minds of big men with guns, after taking small amounts of money to do pretty dastardly things.

Sitting in my office at the embassy, my cellphone buzzed, and the text message from Jim was clear enough: "S-O-S."

I drove across town to the orphanage and made it a few minutes before the police squad.

As they crashed through the front gate with the paddy wagon waiting outside, I walked up to them and detonated my first WMD: a broad smile. "You are most welcome here!" I said, drawing the nearest ones into handshakes and embraces. There may be a natural defense against these aggressive tactics, but they didn't have any.

Then I handed out my business card to each one, asking for theirs in return. "Here is my name. May I know yours?"

The commandant took the Fifth on this, and angrily pushed past me. He unrolled a sealed document that looked like something from Kings Arthur's Court, and began to read aloud. This home for children was to be locked down in the name of something. The Law, I think it was. The children were to be escorted out to the street and left there, end of story.

I had no choice other than to go nuclear: I took out my camera and started filming. The commandant waved me aside and said, "It is forbidden to do that."

I set my little camera on video, and said, "Forbidden under what statute?"

The police squad reached for their weapons, looking to the commandant for orders. I don't want you to think there was anything heroic about this: no Cameroonian policemen would fire on an unarmed foreigner (too much paperwork for them to fill out). The commandant motioned his machine gun toward my camera. So I lowered it. I had all the pictures I needed anyway. He was too spooked to grab for the camera or chip. He didn't know the Geneva Convention texts (nor did I), but he figured they weren't working in his favor.

The resourceful U.S. ambassador meanwhile got wind of what was happening, and called me from the office on my cell phone. He told me, "Put on whoever seems to be in charge."

"A call for you," I said to the commandant. "With compliments, from the U.S. ambassador."

To the commandant my cell phone looked like an angered cobra. He backed away. So did the others.

"Please, Commandant," I said. "The ambassador has some friendly words for you. You wouldn't want to disappoint him."

Reluctantly the commandant took the phone and listened for a couple of minutes. He sweated, anguished, and fumed. Maybe I dramatize slightly, but the message from On High converted the commandant from small bribe taker to a potentially successful defendant in an international child-filching case. Saved by a call. Now Sister Margaret's money was both squandered and valueless.

No one in this scenario was stupid. Not Jim, not Sister Margaret, not the police and their commandant. All played their roles impeccably.

Footnote: Jim got plenty of death threats in the following weeks, but we all knew that the cost of having him popped would exceed Sister Margaret's budget.

I pass on to you for free the survival techniques learned that day, drawing on the wisdom of Sun Tzu: when faced by overwhelming odds, never confront, never retreat, and always leave a way out for the opponent. Following these three simple principles may not guarantee success, but they give you your best chance for making it out alive.

Voice of... Reason
August 3, 2015

There wasn't much to do in Brazzaville in 1980. The little People's Republic of the Congo faces the immense Zaire (the other, capitalist "Congo"), its capital Kinshasa visible in the distance across the mighty Congo River.

I was supposed to be teaching English at the Université Marien Ngouabi, which disdainful expats called "Le Lycée." The Soviets had just invaded Afghanistan, and my classrooms were taken over about half the time for political rallies in favor of the Soviets. The students didn't seem to care much one way or the other. They were affable young people looking for a meal, a job, and a night's sleep. There wasn't much electricity in Brazzaville. They studied like monks, pacing silently with their books at night, reading under the only street lights in the city: the ones on the highway to the airport.

The Pushkin Institute offered free Russian lessons those days, paid by the Soviet embassy. I didn't like what the Soviets were doing outside their borders (or inside, for that matter). But that wasn't the fault of their beautiful language.

The U.S. embassy had directives not to associate with any of the several thousand Soviets in the city. I wasn't part of the embassy, but stopped in anyway to get guidance. The American public affairs officer said, "Well you're a private citizen, so I see no issue with this. If you want to do it, just go ahead."

I showed up at the Pushkin Institute, where the lingua franca was French. I asked if I might take one of their introductory courses. They responded with simple generosity and openness. "Here are your books. The course starts Tuesday."

I said, "I'm a U.S. citizen, if that matters."

"Why would it matter to us?" the kindly registrar said. She handed me a stack of books almost too heavy to carry away on my moped.

The weeks went on and I learned a few words and phrases in my class of six or seven. If any of the students had ulterior motives, they weren't visible. I didn't like the slow pace of my learning, but knew it was only from my own lack of discipline. I was beginning to get the hang of it, and could follow even a few stories. The teachers were astute, and the Institute was a tightly run shop.

The more of the language I learned, the more I saw it as a tall mountain, my own learning curve a small bump on a steep incline. I was keen to learn, but didn't advance as rapidly as I wanted. Plus, the ambient French was an easy fallback when words failed me.

Those were the days when BBC, VOA, Deutsche Welle, Radio Moscow, Radio Netherlands, and others competed head-to-head for attention on short wave channels. Each had an "Africa Service" in English or French, and came on with comforting regularity at news time. VOA was a stitch with its "Special English" (like the joke that ends, "Well in that case, let me tell you… verrryy… sloooowly…").

BBC had the strongest short wave presence locally, and its news programs were dry, professional, reliable, and always on time. Anyone who listened back then will remember with nostalgia the fading and strengthening short wave signal, the artful tuning it took to pick it up solidly, and the lovely English country tune it played to announce news time. And the beep-beep-beep to mark Greenwich Mean Time, now sadly renamed "Universal Time."

Radio Moscow had its biases, but I thought it might help my language learning if I spotted it on the short wave channels. As the story goes, "If you want to learn a language, just go anywhere in the world and find a proselyte. Probably you already know the spiel by heart, so you'll catch on quickly as it comes to you with foreign words." Likewise, Cold War propaganda.

I would listen to BBC at home, sometimes VOA, to get a pretty accurate version of the world's tumults. Then I would try to tune in to Radio Moscow to hear their version of it. I could pick it up pretty easily in its English version, but never quite got the frequency for the original Russian. Curiosity set in, and I wanted to speed up my language learning.

We gathered in the courtyard of the Pushkin Institute after class one afternoon, with students, teachers, and even the director, chatting in French. Russians, Congolese, French, the rare Italian and myself, we were all there to tackle the language from one angle or another.

The Institute director gave me a friendly glance so I said, "I've been trying to find Radio Moscow on the short wave. Would you know the frequency by any chance?" Mind you, this was during a tense period of the Cold War, as the blundering USSR stepped in way over its head in Afghanistan and was later stung badly doing so.

Without hesitation the Institute director said to the fifteen of us gathered in his courtyard, "How would I know? I listen only to the Voice of America."

All laughed and mounted their mopeds to get home before dark.

I think back to the reckless friendliness of the moment, taking a breather from global conflict and differences. Just people in a courtyard. This, I am sure, is how to win hearts and minds, whether you deserve it or not. Way better than repeating a message until it flattens from overuse.

Sometimes He Wondered
August 3, 2015

It's hard not to pick favorites when a satisfying novel gets you into worlds you haven't inhabited. When a good one comes along, it seems to bring its own logic, "proof" of a mathematical process. A zero-head in math, I am an easy victim of fictive manipulations. Show me a clever, false reality and I'll fall for it.

In *And Sometimes I Wonder About You*, Walter Mosley takes us on a gallop through the range of human struggles, which collectively seem like nature's senseless competition for survival. The hilarious and dense haste of it makes you say, "Now, what more is needed? Nothing much." Good fiction gives you both questions and answers, but doesn't tell you how they came.

In his essay "The Art of the Novel," Henry James revealed the way fiction worked for him, using artifice to project reality better than reality can. This is insightful for those of us who are easily affected by the process, though unable to perform it. Aristotle had worked on this, the European Baroque perfected the paradox; simulation is more persuasive than reality, but only in the hands of the magus, the artist.

Do I digress?

In the time of Henry James, people had less time to deal with (life expectancy, for example) whereas in our twenty-first century, we speed through our reflections as if time were just about to run out. Mosley embeds his own elliptical version of the "Art of the Novel" in a single fragment: "He used the knowledge [of reading] he gained to further his understanding of the flaws of humankind."

Not that much of a theory, but in a game of mirrors, Mosley slips out of his fiction for a moment and explains why he writes.

Mosley's worldview is dark and even "noir," but is also a knee-slapping parody of itself. Note the insistence on exactitude of detail and of time. Most of it entirely pointless, to where it doesn't even function to distract or mislead, in case you're trying to figure out "whodunit."

The taxonomy of characters, meant as parodies of Mosley's antecedents, is hilarious and fascinating. Imagine making up names like Mardi Bitterman, Brian "Fat Fudge" Lowman, Sweet Lemon Charles, Alphonse Rinaldo, Camille Esterhouse, and the firm of Lipsky, Van der Calm, Tryman & Wills. Can't we all have such fun? The author does it for us, and makes us willing voyeurs.

Mosley's world, while prizing the noble elements of human yearning, morality, loyalty, love, and hurt, is full also of deadly competition of species in a jungle where only some can survive through cunning, brute strength, libido, and deception. Survival strategies, malice, sadism all commingle with the higher motives to show how Mosley's world really is, not what it would be if it were "better." As the same time, these elements (a defiance of romanticism) are a paint-over of a canvas previously filled. The archaeologist picking up these materials in a time capsule some time from now would not have a prayer of understanding them, since in every step there exists an ironic distance from them and the genres they parody.

See the following for layers of irony we catch instantly, but which would fall flat in a future without context:

> "I have dozens of models. Do you expect me to remember them all?
>
> "I expect, from all my fellow citizens, the same things," I said. "Civility, respect, and honesty. It's rare to receive any of these commodities but I keep hope alive."
>
> "Are you threatening, me, Mr. McGill?"
>
> "If I was, your jaw would already be broken," I said.

And how many jokes can be pulled out of the following onion layers below, once peeled?

> After calling the police, the Professor sat down to his manual typewriter and, with his hands still wet from the blood of his victim, typed a confession starting with the first crime committed against him by Hendricks when he stole the Professor's idea about *Obfuscative Language and the Tyranny of Philosophy*.

The narrator's favorite person, his stepson Twill, gets a terse introduction in which strength and economy of expression give us a hundred verses of prosody:

> Twill is five-ten, slender, handsome, and dark as our West African ancestors before the slave ships came. There was a small scar just under his lower lip, a reminder of folk heroes like Achilles and Cain.

Fiction hardly gets better. When the narrator's groin becomes the center of attention, he says all that's needed, no more or less:

> I didn't resent her power any more than a bear resents the warmth of the sun waking him from a blissful hibernation.

Mosley shows off virtuosity; that is what artists do. Modesty is not a virtue here. He taunts his predecessors: "I can do anything you could do, better."

Whenever I think I've found a favorite fiction, another comes along to outdo it. Mosley tells us little about history or social order, but shares enough about his view of it to draw us into his world of artifice:

> A man of my age losing love, or some adjacent emotion, was somewhere beyond grief.
> Life was like a rat's maze tended by some insane god that tortured and shepherded us for some reason he (or maybe she) could no longer remember.

These are powerful sentiments, indicating despair and a world fallen apart. Mosley may be exteriorizing genuine disappointments, but it doesn't matter if he is just yanking our chain. The delight flows, either way.

Mosley's narrator comes alive because of so many contrasts (tenderness, brute strength, a suppressed but active super-ego, the ability and need to capture love) – not only expecting the worst of life, but also taken aback when finding the best:

> Marella Herzog, a woman with a dog whistle that could call out the best in me. I felt that if I could spend a week in her company I might grow back a full head of hair.

The versatility is a joke on us, because the contrasts exaggerate normal life. But departure (not "escape") from the normal is what drives the thrill of artifice, and renders us grateful to those able to dupe us. We love to be fooled.

Take this, future archaeologists:

> My knuckles and cheekbone were both throbbing to the beat of my heart. *That's life*, said the Buddha and Sinatra.

The packing of oblique references in twenty words is ours alone, like the sea shell we ourselves found on the beach, and you never will.

Zephyra Ximenez, Paulie DeGeorges, Evangeline Sidney-Gray, Tolstoy ("Trot") McGill, Julius Sneed, and the blunt spondee of Josh Farth. These cadences evoke the dense populkatnios of a Balzac or Faulkner. Frankly they outdo Raymond Chandler's by being funnier.

Thank you, Walter Mosley, for the fun and fascination. Thanks especially for giving us your real opinion of your character Luke Nye:

> …[who] passed for a black man but who actually looked to be a direct descendant of the moray eel.

There They Go Again
August 12, 2015

This thing called the "international community" rises to clown-like behavior when Haiti holds elections. They always did, and I hope they'll give it up one day.

After six murders, scores of beatings, and one third of the ballots trashed in the streets, Haiti's legislative elections August 9 were pronounced "a success" by the UN, Brazil, France, Canada, Spain, the United States, the EU, and the OAS. Read: "Good enough for Haitians."

CARICOM, which sometimes opines on these things, apparently decided to sit this one out, much to their credit. Election observers acted heroically and thoroughly, but their bosses ignored the data with their pre-cooked, phony reports.

Behind these shoddy standards is an underlying racism that was once well pointed out by former Assistant Secretary for Latin America (no left winger!) Roger Noriega. Inferior people, inferior elections.

Let's call them collectively the Internats. They observed and photographed the trashing of the electoral process, but decided Haiti had to move on. This gives every encouragement to those who cheated, murdered, and beat up voters, to do so again and again, since no one in the Internats ever seems to object. Better not to send observers, than to bless criminality and leave the Haitian voters once again bullied not only by ambient thugs within, but indifferent patricians looking in from the outside.

The same happened in the disastrous elections of 2000 (a series of three.) After the first one, Haitian voters saw the jig was up as CBC filmed their votes being tossed into the Caribbean while observers said, in effect, Haitian votes need not be counted. Smiley face back then, and Haitian voters just chose to sit out the following two elections, with a lethal ruling party's thumb heavily on the scale, and opposition candidates killed and jailed for having the audacity of being candidates. Haitians may be unfortunate, but they are not stupid.

The Internats do not speak for me. If laziness and denial were their motives, it would be understandable. But contempt for voters just doesn't match the now long-empty words calling for democratization in all countries.

After the nasty elections in Burundi last month, the U.S. government issued a "strong" statement using the word "warn" with respect to self-appointed autocrat du jour Pierre Nkurunziza. The European Union and the African Union made real statements, saying they would "not recognize" the Burundi elections. Guess which Internat postings got the notice of the media?

One longs for the days of PJ Crowley, when actual statements were beginning to come out of the U.S. government, to its credit, and when USG statements began to say what they meant and mean what they said. Today's tea leaf readers, wholly disregarded by world observers but enamored of their own tautologies, evidently mastered self-delusion. By the time their words were disregarded in international media, other issues had become more pressing. It's called "OBE," Overtaken by Events.

I am not picking on the U.S. government here, just pointing out that its statements no longer capture attention as they did, say, in the era of Ralph Bunche. Now we draw on his masterful vocabulary, which used to keep a tenuous peace in the Middle East in the 1950s. But the same words no longer have much effect because we are no longer, well, Ralph Bunche. The credibility behind a government's words count more than the word selection, and by far. We are deficient in the former, and spinning our wheels with the latter.

Please have a look at this little *cri de coeur*, then tell me: was this an election the Internats should have endorsed?

Watch out: legislative runoffs and first-round presidential elections come October 25. Maybe.

Overnight to Ystad
August 13, 2015

The fate of Denmarks's Jews in October 1943 was an anecdote in a sea of malice. My Danish friend Michael was on one of those boats, the ones wandering around in the Øresund on a dark night in October, lights out lest the Nazi patrols find them, and also lost in an autumn storm, headed possibly for Sweden, but also possibly to Poland or Germany itself.

I asked Michael how it was that night, and he said, "I was two months old."

I said, "Make an effort," but stubbornly he couldn't remember what happened, so instead at breakfast the next morning a book landed at my breakfast place, the panoramic study *Countrymen*, by Bo Lidegaard, the editor in chief of Danish daily *Politiken* (London: Atlantic Books, 2015).

After reading it on the flight home to Washington, I see there was much more to the rescue than I'd thought – more disconnected circumstance, timing, opportunism all around, and dumb luck. Knowing more now than I did, I admire Danes more, not less.

A cipher in an infinity of dashed hopes, the 7,000 saved did well for themselves, communicated and chronicled the event, and their countrymen did well by them also.

Even so, I had never before made the connection between the date and the rescue. By late 1943, the Nazi invasion of the Soviet Union was already going badly, and many in Europe thought the nightmare would soon be over. Nazis were already thinking ahead to the reckoning which later had a name: Nuremberg. No "good" Nazis I guess, but they were not fools. They knew they would end up twisting on meat hooks either if they failed to do Berlin's bidding or if they did so and were captured by the Allies afterward.

Navigating between these two consequences was not easy, and some of them did so very ably. Some get "credit" for looking the other way as Danish fishermen packed their boats and stole away in the autumn night for Sweden on the other side. In the case of the commercial attaché at the German embassy in Copenhagen, Georg Ferdinand Duckwitz, it seemed there was genuine revulsion for the actions of his Nazi bosses in arranging roundups despite promises to the contrary. He went to tip off the Danish Socialist Party of the date of the roundup (no, it wasn't the local rabbi). But might he have done so with the knowledge of the commanding civilian Nazi on the scene, Werner Best, protégé and confidant of one Heinrich Himmler? Duckwitz certainly did this at risk of his life, and maybe of Best's as well, but did both have a stake in their escape from prosecution after war's end?

This is one of the more intriguing conundrums of the drama. And of course people behave more interestingly in dramas, under stress, and that is why we have movies and plays. If these were no-brainers, they wouldn't have happened.

Other variables I hadn't really focused on earlier: we know that Herr Hitler loved Scandinavians, and in particular Denmark's king, Christian X. Hitler kept courting Christian, who in return only displayed his contempt for the upstart sadist and said so very openly – one of the few Europeans to get away with such a thing. When Christian was recovering in the hospital from a nasty fall from a horse, the Führer sent a get-well telegram to the king. The famous reply ("Herr Hitler, my only regret is that you are not here [in the hospital] with me") was a verbal finger that only Scandinavian royalty could pull off or survive. And no, the king did not "wear" the Star of David in the streets of Copenhagen (urban legend) but he did say at a meeting, "Well, if they must wear them, then I guess we all must do so."

Yet another variable which made this odd confabulation possible: while the neutral Swedes had behaved badly in 1940-41 in offering their train system for Hitler's invasion of Norway, and supplying the famous "Big Bertha" for the Nazi weapons arsenal, it seems they switched course as a nation in the following two years, and were extremely gracious and welcoming to any refugee who made it to their shores. All eyewitness accounts seem to corroborate this. Was this their better angels coming out, or a cold calculation of how things would shake out after war's end, or just decency getting the upper hand? It seemed the latter.

And yet more peculiarities I hadn't fully considered before: The Hitlerian presence in Denmark was neither by invasion nor Anschluss, but by something called "cooperation" (*samarbeitet*). Danes knew they could not oppose Nazism alone, and reasonably enough submitted to the inevitable. They even accepted responsibility for policing their own country, and yet the police were wholly uncooperative when it came to persecuting any of their fellow countrymen without due process. The Nazis could count on local cooperation in racial eradication in most European countries. But in Denmark, while anti-Semitism lay under the surface, so did the countervailing force of reason ("If they round *them* up, we could be next") and an embedded veneration of rule of law. The oldest surviving parliamentary documents in the world, after all, are to this day in the Faroe Islands, which were and are part of the Danish realm. Nazis were not about to kill their favorite Aryans, but their cat-and-mouse games at making everything appear legal just didn't work at all with Danes. Local police were trained to keep things by the book, not by superior forces from the outside.

As the Eastern Front went badly, Berlin could not afford to divert troops to subdue an upstart state. Berlin was well advised by Werner Best that Danes would be unreliable in a roundup, and would be unmanageable if their local rules or culture were trampled. The timing just wasn't right for Berlin to pay attention to anything much else than killing as many Russians as they could during that brutal winter, which went about as well for Hitler as it had gone for Napoleon 131 years earlier.

In all of Europe, only Denmark and Bulgaria saved their persecuted countrymen. Denmark had the luck of having a friendly, neutral country just a few kilometers away.

The rescue did not take place during a single night, as I'd thought, but over a period of three weeks. Lots of occupiers saw this happening, and they did catch a few hundred unfortunates. But Best reported cunningly to Berlin after the rescue to Sweden that "The Jewish question in Denmark has been settled." Meaning: none in sight. He skillfully omitted what Berlin probably knew: they hadn't been killed, just sort of disappeared.

No one at the time had any misunderstanding of what happened to people who were evacuated on trains to Treblinka. The idea that someone in Washington just wasn't aware is just a silly historic platitude.

It's hard to put oneself in the mental state of someone learning they would soon be rounded up and killed, or that of the fisherman and boat owners and Danish police, ambulance drivers, nurses, hospital clerks, Lutheran clergy, who all in fact worked together to foil the roundup. Did they really have to go? And if so, was there any chance of making it out alive?

The initial disbelief that Werner Best would actually lie to Danish political leaders was understandable enough. Also, the genuine fear of the boatmen, who assumed Nazi patrol boats would come and sweep up all of them, then execute the rescuers and rescued both. So it doesn't seem that greed was the main motivator behind fisherman taking payments of 500-1500 kroner per passenger, when in fact no one was left behind for lack of cash. The richer paid for the poorer, and anyway, the boats needed to refuel on the Swedish side to make it back home.

So in many ways the story is an Andersen fairy tale, only one that in fact occurred. Bravos to all involved – except maybe the infamous "Gestapo-Juhl," the Nazi officer who kept blundering on stage to spoil the party and actually round up Jews. He was a bit tone deaf even to his own colleagues. Any fairy tale needs a good (and stupid) villain to spice up the story.

The problem comes with history itself. Denmark was lucky that fall, for the variables above. Additionally, they met their good luck with exceedingly good and admirable behavior.

But history is not static. All things change, with reliable randomness. Sentiments which were once lethal return with blander faces, narratives, and intentions.

The Danish People's Party (*Dansk Folkeparti, DF*) now rules the nation with its founder, Pia Kjæsgaard, serving as Denmark's equivalent of speaker of the house and embedded with the Liberal Party (*Venstre*) in a coalition with Venstre's Lars Løkke Rasmussen as prime minister. DF's anti-immigration policy, sometimes compared to France's National Front under Marine Le Pen, has minded its vocabulary and successfully sues those who call it "nationalist." So I won't. They won the European Parliament election in 2014 with almost 27 percent of the Danish vote – the largest percentage of any Danish party. In 2015 they got 21 percent of the vote in the Danish general election, doubled their seats in the Folketing.

No, history does not "repeat" itself. This is a horrible canard and makes arguments ("Munich!") for the most foolish of policies. But it does seem to indicate that disdain for lessons of the past remains a big factor in democracies, and likely always will.

Ruthless
August 17, 2015

In her August 16 column in the *Washington Post*, Ruth Marcus paraphrases Carly Fiorina from 2008, saying something positive about Hillary Clinton. This doesn't affect my life much to begin with. But then in addition I see quotation marks and the words, punctiliously noted from seven years ago, "That's off the record."

Wow, reminds me of the Wild West days of Spanish journalism of the early 1990s, when scribes would quote embassy officials of various countries, "…and he said, off the record [sic], 'Yes no maybe…'" I remember helping one journalist find someone to quote back then, and then never being forgiven (me!) because of the offending violation of basic rules of decency.

I guess this is what passes for investigative reporting these days.

Marcus gives an expansive explanation of two hundred words (one third of her column) of why it is ethical to quote someone who has said "off the record." Seems like a bit of sophistry. Something about Fiorina (not a Columbia Journalism School grad, and why should she be?) saying "off the record" *after* the quotable remark instead of *before*.

Marcus says her purpose here is to catch a presidential candidate saying something inconsistent seven years ago with what she's saying now.

Would this be a sample of our hifalutin political dialogue of summer 2015? I don't know what the baseball analogy would be, but something like swinging and missing. The only real reasons for writing this stuff would be (I guess) either harming a person by tricking them at a game they aren't meaning to play, or possibly calling in bragging rights for having had a conversation once with someone who now has a 0.251 per cent chance of moving into the White House in January of 2017. Pretty tawdry either way. Possibly there was a deadline breathing down Marcus's back and this was a solution to writer's block.

I'm glad that Jeff Bezos has kept good to his word in not affecting the editorial style or content of the *Washington Post* when he bought it some months ago. I was getting used to the many typos in the *Post* and in all the wire services, which I read daily and forgive, because I'm more interested in following different accounts of the current dramas of the human race than I am in spelling and semicolons. But, but… sputter. I'm not angry really, just taken aback at what one crab in barrel will do to crawl a bit higher than the next one.

Actually, really it's more like selling a car to an innocent and saying, "You wanted wheels, too? You should have said so."

If Marcus's purpose is to discredit Candidate Fiorina, that should be easy enough by taking any of Fiorina's recent intended quotes, which in my book are pretty crude and objectionable. Judging a person by what they mean to say, and what they do, seems like a pretty straight game, without descending to tricks when they're not even needed.

Ruth Marcus, I forgive you and I'll continue reading you because you often produce very good copy. But my-o, note to self: don't take calls from this person. She'll quote you seven years later from the inner rings in the tree trunk. Rules exist for a reason; you don't get to rewrite them every time just to get some attention to the detriment of another. Even (and especially) in a climate of vulgarity, people who already have our attention should rise above.

The Great James Baker

August 23, 2015

I'm not talking about policy here. We may have had a more skillful secretary of state, but I if so, I don't know who it might have been. Ben Franklin? Dean Acheson? Possibly, but Baker could hold his own with any of them.

He wasn't especially friendly or affable. That wasn't his job. He didn't mind if people didn't like him; he was there to do the work, and did so. He worked hand in glove with his boss, George H. W. Bush, and got along fine with his Soviet counterpart, Eduard Shevardnadze, as his boss did with Gorbachev. History will give credit to those four for finding a way out of the Cold War. Never mind what came next; that was another department.

In the fall of 1991, we got six days' notice in Madrid that we would run a Middle East Peace Conference there. The first we heard of this was Spanish Prime Minister Felipe González announcing it in Tel Aviv in late October. We were blindsided and lots of colleagues were on fall vacation at the time.

In the Madrid of those days, it took an average of 18 months to install a phone line in a home, but somehow we had to put in 7,000 of them for the press on six days' notice. I can't take credit for any of that, but I remember Madrileños weeping in public: "They put in 7,000 lines in two days; I'm still waiting for mine since 1989."

I was sent to the Royal Palace, the venue of the talks, mainly just to shuttle TV tapes from inside the negotiating hall to motorcycles waiting outside in the street, to rush the footage to network uplinks so it could go out on newscasts. Never mind Internet links, this was long before things became so simple.

I was something less than a fixture, but I was inside the room when the negotiations got underway October 30. Lots of Middle East peace meetings had failed, but this was "post-Oslo," so there was some hope something might come of it this time. There was cautious optimism all around. We knew that none of the parties wanted to be there, but also that James A. Baker had forced them, one by one, into the room by persuasion and a little intimidation behind the scenes. I think all the negotiators wanted the talks to fail, but no one wanted to be the one to blame if they did.

The Great Baker had gotten them together and clutched them in his bullying embrace. I remember him with his hands stretched out on the table in front of him, head poised like a reptile about to strike, glaring at every delegate individually with intense eye contact. He looked like a pterodactyl about to pounce and kill. A fearful silence took over the room. Only Baker could pull this off.

After a very intimidating silence, he said to all, his reptilian eye darting to each negotiator one at a time, "Very well, we have brought you together." Long silence. "We have begun the dialogue." Long silence. "And if you accomplish nothing..." Long silence. "...You will have only yourselves to blame."

Maybe the negotiators in the room were used to this sort of head cracking, but I found it terrifying. And indeed, moral terror and dialogue traps may be the only solution, if ever there is to be one, for the intractable Crescent.

Middle Easterners have always outsmarted us, as they did that week in 1991. The Syrian delegation threatened to walk out, but were persuaded off site, with a personal stimulus package waved across their palms, to stay. As the week came to its end, the negotiators seemed to fall into an unusual fraternity: all had the same interest, which was to get out from under the shadow of the Pterodactyl.

Baker was long gone before the Israeli Premier Shamir figured out how to outmaneuver the others – though any one of them might have done the same.

On Friday morning, Shamir said, "As you all know, the Jewish Sabbath comes tonight, so religious law obliges me to be at home before the sun sets today. So, gentlemen and ladies, I must now say farewell."

The Muslims in the room were livid at the ploy, knowing they might have played the same card 24 hours earlier, but hadn't thought to do so.

Baker had brought the scorpions and frogs all in the same room at the same time. No mean feat. Nothing much was accomplished that week, but no one else could have gotten as far as he did. And as he had said insightfully, it turned out not to be his fault.

Cable to Nowhere
August 24, 2015

Contrary to a generosity of spirit in America, both our political parties have shown disdain for the underdog in foreign policy, kicking them in the teeth when empathy might be more in character. Bipartisan annoyance at the suffering of foreigners seems to twin our Left and Right.

Faced with the slaughter of a million Biafrans in 1967-70, Lyndon Johnson sided forcefully with Nigeria's central government, saying of the Biafrans, "Get those [n…] children off my television set."

Only a couple of years later, President Nixon, presented with wide-scale massacres in what is now Bangladesh, said of Indian attempts to staunch the bloodletting, "The Indians are a slippery, treacherous people." He wanted unblemished relations with the West Pakistan aggressors, who became his go-between with Zhou Enlai's China.

In both cases, the U.S. government was enamored of the status quo, which in one instance held firm (Biafra/Nigeria) and in the other yielded a new nation which might have been favorably inclined to us if we had even politely asked the West Pakistanis under President Yahya to attenuate the slaughter. We didn't.

Dacca (now Dhaka)'s U.S. consul general, Archer Blood, sent a famous telegram challenging Washington's passivity in the face of genocide. Written as a dissent channel cable by Blood's subordinates, the text got Blood's approval and even an extra paragraph from him to strengthen the point. All involved knew that Washington vindictiveness under Nixon and Kissinger would come down on the signers' careers in the Foreign Service. Short-term risk, long-term gain.

Nothing comparable in grandeur, we did a dissent channel cable in Port-au-Prince in 2000, when Washington directives came almost daily, instructing us at the embassy to find ways of making President Jean-Bertrand Aristide somehow look and smell good. It wasn't easy, because in this case there weren't really even pigs' lips to put lipstick on. Both U.S. political parties (2000, 2001) found ways to wed themselves to Haiti's ruling party as the latter killed opposition leaders, tortured journalists, locked down the local economy, set the capital on fire twice weekly, and went out of its way to thumb its nose at the U.S. and other potentially friendly governments. It also stole so much money that when some mountains of it were retrieved in Aristide's basement after his departure in 2004, it was too sticky with mold to save, and had to be burned.

In Washington, we at the embassy in Port-au-Prince were code-named "Captain Bly" because we were seen as mutinous.

To us, the State Department Haiti desk was known as "Mother," because they called us every day to make sure we were behaving. The embassy staff was of varied and even conflicting backgrounds and political stripes, but we had eyes and ears, and all saw that the local regime's malice was too obvious to ignore. We knew that Washington's daily orders to make it seem better must have had some realpolitik logic behind it, but none of us could see any short- or long-term benefit in putting up with it. In this case it wasn't a tribe or ideology or religion at the receiving end of daily human rights abuses, but nearly every Haitian. People were dirt poor as ever, but now also afraid, hungry, deracinated, and disillusioned, especially after the three sham elections of 2000.

We were witnesses; we knew about Good Samaritan laws in some U.S. states requiring people to try to stop a crime if they saw it *in flagrante*.

A colleague and I talked about it, and decided to go the dissent channel route. U.S. law (not to mention morality) trumped loyalty in an adverse and extreme situation. The dissent channel cable, like affirmative action, was instituted under the Nixon administration, the one you might least expect. It was set up after Vietnam to allow U.S. diplomats to vent in cases where their own chief of mission demurred to Washington's directives. Dissents never changed policy much, but they allowed individuals to skewer themselves by registering disapproval of the orders we were getting from the "thousand-mile screwdriver" from Washington.

I drafted a dissent text arguing that the current regime in Haiti was aggressively persecuting its own people, and asking the U.S. government to lower its level of unconditional love for it, at least to make public statements denouncing murder as an instrument of domestic policy in Haiti. Even bland comments were blunted by Washington.

Drafting and editing were a cinch. Then it occurred to me that our chargé d'affaires was not a bad guy at all, and deserved the courtesy of seeing the message before we sent it out. My colleague agreed.

Unruffled, the chargé read it and said, "Why would this go out as a dissent, when we all see it the same way? If you want, we can send this as a front-channel cable under my name." Kind of like Archer Blood in Dacca, thirty years before. He smiled.

My colleague and I were non-plussed. In signing the cable, our chargé would be sticking his neck way out and offering himself as a lightning rod for Washington's wrath.

"In fact, let's send this around to Country Team and see what they say."

The text went around to the consular officer, the political and economic officers, USAID and all the others. With a few minor edits, it got unanimous sign-ons.

None of this did a jot to U.S. policy toward Haiti, nor does this anecdote compare in grandeur to the Blood Telegram. But the process was the same in underlings rising up, and their courageous boss in agreement, willing to take the brunt of Washington backlash.

Like demographic growth of the human race, the U.S. electorate's interest in foreign policy was negligible for the longest time (usually less than five per cent of what "factored" into the voting process). Now with humanitarian crises more visible, terrorism, a global economy locked in possible meltdown, and climate change denial, foreign policy may begin to rise on the graph. If so, Americans should look to their own inner core of empathy for the underdog, and see about breaking a pattern of bedazzlement with the status-quo-no-matter-what.

Potato, Potahto, Monogamy, Polygamy
August 28, 2015

Five of us sat at a lunch restaurant at a fishing village in Massachusetts, I think Cohasset. You can't find a more congenial setting.

Three of them came from sub-Saharan Africa, one from Tunisia. All were jurists on a study tour of the American court system. The Tunisian had been haranguing the three others for two weeks, proselytizing monogamy for their countries. They would have none of it. Polygamy suited them just fine. No woman was present to argue the other side. Nor, said one of the sub-Saharan Africans, would they if they had the chance.

In the 1970s, the good citizens of Maghreb countries condescended, patronized, cajoled their neighbors in countries to the south. They saw the Sahara as the dividing line between civilization and paganism, though no one used those terms exactly. Each time the Tunisian in the group opened his mouth to take up the same cause (over and over) the others would ignore him or start an animated conversation on another topic.

New England clam chowder came, and the Tunisian made one last go of it. "Tunisia, the Switzerland of North Africa, is on excellent terms with Europe, and partly because of our laws forbidding polygamy. You could do the same, and you'll see tourism and trade come in as a result."

The others looked sadly into their soup as if into dark chambers of sulfurous elements. Why spoil a perfect spring day? they seemed to think.

Ignoring hints as always, the Tunisian pressed on: "Here is how you do it. Just get a test case, find a plaintiff, and work the process up the line until it reaches your Supreme Court. Then you rule by precedent. You'll see; it will work."

The Malian, at the end of his tether, put down his soup spoon with some clatter. He glared at the Tunisian, embolded by the supportive ennui of his two other colleagues.

"In Mali," he said, "I AM the Supreme Court."

No more words on that topic for the rest of the tour, and the Tunisian gave up his proselytizing. "And that," as Virginia Woolf said at the end of her short story "Lapin and Lapinova," "was the end of that marriage."

Homicide Fine, Fax Not So Good

August 30, 2015

Time to move into the NEC—the New Embassy Compound—in Yaoundé, Cameroon. One medium-sized African post was blessed by the Overseas Building Office (OBO) with a spanking new, $40 million building, the most handsome structure in the country and an object of admiration all around.

The town was as atwitter as we were for our escape at last from our temporary digs in the grubby downtown area. No regrets for the old maze of buildings sort-of connected by steps, staircases, heavy metal doors, and a sometimes lethal busy street in front.

We were uplifted to do the move, though our colleagues in the communications office warned that if OBO forgot to put cooling units, the server and router rooms, our email and phones and fax would probably never work. Plenty of messages to Washington, but OBO went ahead with their plans. We believed our communications colleagues, but no number of cables to OBO in Washington got them to do the right thing and install the cooling units.

The day came for the NEC opening. Our inspired ambassador

thought to stage a ribbon-cutting ceremony at the *old* building site, symbolically showing that the closed off street downtown would revert back to the city, and traffic could flow once again. We got TV cameras ready, lined up taxis at both ends of the old embassy block. As the master of ceremonies, on cue I said into a loudspeaker, "Gentlemen, you may now pass." Three taxis from each side of the street proceed through a previously closed area, showing it was now liberated for public use. It wasn't much of a cymbal crash, but anyway it was on video tape for the local TV.

The day after our move, a gruesome murder took place at the local American school, in front of a hundred traumatized students ten to fifteen years old. One pupil took a knife and beheaded another – well, mostly severed the head, not completely, just enough to leave the other one very bleeding and very dead. I can provide more detail if someone wants it.

This was not an ideological act, but an impulsive reaction to some weeks of gay-baiting. Talk about bullying on campus!

Everyone in the city wanted to know what had happened, why it happened, how a young student managed to get a kitchen knife onto campus, and so on. There was a legal connection between the American school and embassy, so we had to put out a statement. It was not a good day.

I was in an elegant new office with a lovely view of a hill and some pleasing spaces within. However, because of the structural flaws our communications colleagues had foreseen, there was no usable telephone, fax, or email.

I walked a handwritten draft statement around the building, to get colleagues' clearance. We had to provide some facts to the public about the grisly homicide at the school, even if there wasn't much good to say about it.

Once we all agreed on a final version of the statement, I lifted the phone to call the local TV stations, but there was no phone line. I tried calling on my cell phone, but the elegant, thick NEC walls blocked the signal. So I stepped outside with my handwritten text and cell phone and managed to reach the local TV station.

"I have a statement on the American school homicide," I said to the editor.

"We surely appreciate it," said the desk editor. "You will need to send it to us by fax on embassy letterhead."

"I'm afraid we have no printer and no fax," I said.

"Impossible," said the editor. "You say you are the U.S. Embassy. Of course you have a fax."

"Truly not," I said "We temporarily lost it during our embassy move."

"Sorry," the editor said. "Strict network policy. We have no other way of verifying that you are who you say you are. Standards to maintain, you know."

Stumped. I understood the TV needed procedures, but I wasn't able to comply. The TV editor was not very sympathetic, and reasonably enough stuck to the protocol. After all, the U.S. government had spent $40 million on a building and should have the foresight to get its messaging right.

I took the handwritten note, put an embassy seal on it, and walked it into the TV station at the other end of town. On this basis, they accepted it. We could say that the homicide that day went fine, but there were obstructions in what went out to the public. The router cooler came in by air the next week, and within ten days we looked and behaved like an embassy. It's always bad to have a homicide on your home turf, but if only this one could have come a couple of weeks later.

"Mister Bratton, I Presume?"
September 7, 2015

Michael Bratton is all over the news since July 22, when at age 67, he said he would bow out as NYPD Commissioner should Bill de Blasio win a second term as mayor. De Blasio, a bigger man in every sense than Rudy Giuliani, gets the backs of brooding New York police officers, but has only praise for his commissioner. He doesn't begrudge people's love for his commissioner as Rudy did. De Blasio says if Pope Francis can serve into his seventies, then why can't Mike Bratton? Granted, the mission and lifestyle are not exactly the same.

During Bratton's tempestuous times with Giuliani in 1994-96, he invented something called "broken window policing," and encouraged his police on their beats to pursue any offense, like turnstile jumping in the subway. Crime plummeted – especially violent crime. From two thousand homicides in New York in 1990, the figure has dropped in 2014 to 300 (the lowest figure since 1963.) New York is now "the tenth safest of the big cities" in the United States.

Compare East Saint Louis, with twenty-one times the homicides of the national average.

Now, even Bratton says there is much mystery in this. Cause-and-effect? Coincidence? Perhaps having the largest prison population in the world—both numerically and proportionately—may have relieved the United States of troublemakers, though God knows many dolphins were taken in by the tuna traps in this vast series of holding cells for people of color and a few others.

Ken Auletta did a superb profile in the September 7 *New Yorker*, arching back to Bratton's start as a traffic cop in Cambridge, Massachusetts, at the age of one and a half, when he went to the street for fun to direct cars, until his father scooped him up in his arms and took him back home.

Michael Bratton is a walking lightning rod, hailed by many, feared by many, despised by some. His motives seem to be pretty simple: make it possible for citizens in a vast city to do what they have to do in their lives, without the layer of fear they once had to go anywhere, at any time.

As we used to say in evaluating junior officers in the Foreign Service, "He did not prevent a good thing from happening." This was our snarky way of saying it is difficult to figure out who gets credit when a good thing happens. We never really wrote that phrase; we just said it during coffee breaks.

After Giuliani fired Bratton in 1996 (apparently from jealousy, as Bratton's programs were working for the City and Giuliani's were not), Bratton went into the private consulting business, and was even approached by the government of the United Kingdom for advice on how to deal with crime in its major cities. He was yet to head out to Los Angeles to be commissioner there, 2002-09.

During his waiting period, among other things he came to South Africa, where he was hailed as a god, or conquering hero, for his zero-tolerance approach. This would have been in 1997 or '98. All South Africans lived in fear of violent crime in a country where homicide, rape, and domestic violence were off the charts. No ethnic group was immune, and even the rich lived behind electrified barbed wire fences. Everyone with a car carried a hunting knife near the front seat. Carjackings were so common that when someone came up with a flame thrower device, controlled from the steering wheel and capable of incinerating anyone who approached the driver's side from the street, the constabulary of South Africa tolerated the practice. Even the judiciary found this an acceptable form of self-defense.

I was Bratton's guide for a couple of days during his visit to Pretoria and Johannesburg. As rapturous headlines blazed, he became something like the Holy Shrine of Lourdes: "Touch me and you will be cured."

I decided Bratton should meet South Africa's finest prosecutor, Jan d'Oliveira. D'Oliveira had braved many death threats in going after perpetrators of racial violence – mainly white-on-black. He had nailed a good number of them even in the pre-Mandela period, performing unlikely acts of heroism and astute and relentless prosecutions.

Just three of us in the room. I don't think Bratton would resent this bit of revelation about a private moment, but in any case I don't know how to reach him for comment.

Bratton and d'Oliveira took an immediate liking for each other; they worked different sides of the justice equation, but both passionately believed in making it work, so as to have societies worth living in. Like a boxer and a wrestler in a good-natured contest, they didn't know exactly how to go about it at the beginning of their meeting. They asked about each other's families and training, and quickly they knew they were of the same professional mold. This was one of those "Great Meetings," like Isaiah Berlin's night talking with Anna Akhmatova in Leningrad, the sort of thing that goes down in history without the details ever being known.

Seeing the vast possibilities for information exchange between two consummate professionals, Bratton asked d'Oliveira at one point, "And how do you deal with juries?"

With a sly smile, d'Oliveira said, "In South Africa we don't have juries."

Bratton savored this fact during a long moment of silence. It seemed too good to be true, like having a horse with legal hormones in the race, bound to win every time and yet with no one to challenge the vast advantage it had over the others. There was envy, joy, contentment, admiration, disbelief that any place in the world could have such a manageable justice system which actually made it possible for a prosecutor to do his/her job. It was startling and satisfying to see a man with such joy in his face.

D'Oliveira did not gloat, but understood Bratton's moment of astonishment and the latter's belief that he had been afforded a moment's visit in Heaven.

Bratton went on to be on every TV show and in every newspaper in South Africa, a country hungry for crime reduction and an innate love of zero tolerance, though they knew little of its consequences and downsides, such as massive incarceration rates and public discomfort with the police.

Violent crime is indeed down in the United States. Result or unrelated anecdote? Michael Bratton has had the honesty never to take full credit for causation of zero tolerance, though he has maintained the policy in Los Angeles and now again in New York, where he returned as commissioner in 2014. On July 14 of this year, after the death of Eric Garner on Staten Island, he advised his 35,000 cops to use more restraint. The minority population of New York and other cities went to the streets when Garner's killer went unindicted. No easy answers, with innocents being hurt alternately by crazed human felines and overreacting constabularies.

What we do know is that, with two hundred million guns in the country in the hands of who-knows-who and who-knows-where, police have reason to be scared of their shadows. Who wouldn't be? As Bratton himself said in his op/ed of January 23, "To rebuild trust, a little graciousness can go a long way."

"Je m'en vais"

September 11, 2015

Big news! Thomas Yayi Boni will be president of the Republic of Benin until 2016. This is worthy of respect, gratitude, and archival notation.

Oh, and did I mention? He will step down in 2016 at the end of his second, democratically elected five-year mandate. This is huge.

Citizens in countries governed by African presidents like Jammeh, Gnassingbe, Sassou Nguesso, Chissano, Nkurunziza, Mugabe, Biya, Kabila, Obiang, dos Santos, Museveni, al-Bashir, Deby, and Isaias (not to mention those of other continents) would think they had died and gone to heaven if their leaders did something likewise. Gabon's Omar Bongo relinquished power after forty-one years, but only after his death. Even then he was reluctant to let go, and only to his son Ali Bongo.

Barack Obama invited four democratically-elected African leaders to the White House July 29, 2011, as a gesture of encouragement for the democratic process in Africa. Presidents Condé of Guinea, Issoufou of Niger, and Ouattara of Côte d'Ivoire joined Yayi in the

White House to receive thanks from the world's second-largest democracy for being among a tiny coalition of the democratic willing on the African continent. It seems the invitation had its intended effect, along with President Obama's 2009 speech in Accra ("Africa does not need strong men, it needs strong institutions") and at the African Union in July of 2015.

This is, I mean, NEWSWORTHY. You won't see much written about it, and I'm not whining for more "good news" on Africa, as I don't believe in good being better than true. This man Yayi said at the Atlantic Council in Washington September 10, *"Je m'en vais,"* I will go. He knew he would get rapturous applause at this audience, and well deserved it when it came. Just going. What a tremendous gift to a country, and how seldom the world's ruling gangsters seem to muster the courage for that singular act.

I remember Benin in the bad days of the 1970s under a brain-dead Maoist regime, when people were sent to prison and worse for neglecting to say "Ready for the Revolution!" when answering the phone. The stiflers had their days of joy, but they were numbered, as all inactive, repressive regimes are, sooner or later.

No one expected it, but the dictator du jour Mathieu Kérékou (a great role model for democracy) actually conceded power to Nicéphone Soglo in 1991 after a true election. Kérékou wanted to return, but by legitimate means, and did so in 2001. But both were disqualified in 2006 for age and for, well, professional longevity, paving the way for the current Thomas Yayi Bono. Yayi got religion and is committed to leaving after this two terms are up – no constitutional amendments, no president for life, no "Who else but me could do this job?" This is inspirational, and should serve as a model for next-door dictator Gnassingbé (aka Egadéma) in Togo. Gnassingbé's predecessor (and father), Gnassingbé Eyadéma ("Eyadémerde" to his countrymen) did no service to his country or the cause of democracy by deluding himself to be indispensable. At least the son has a master's degree from George Washington University, and had a lengthy trial period as president during twenty days in 2005 just to see if he would like the job.

September 8 Joe Biden signed a second compact with the Republic of Benin, for $375 million, for the development of energy sources including solar, wind, and off-grid generators, to give the majority of Béninois hope of getting electricity in their lifetime. One hour off the grid equals three hours without water. Sadly the U.S. government's "Power Africa" program has been more bluster than delivery, but the idea was good when President Obama and USAID Director Rajiv Shah launched it in 2014. Not much money for this noble purpose, but anyway…

The Millennium Challenge Corporation, founded in 2004 under President George W. Bush, is the only development model by the U.S. government that has worked. Using guidelines from third-party sources (World Bank, Transparency International, IMF…), the MCC awards "compacts" to only a handful of countries which meet minimum criteria of decent governance, controllable corruption, vigorous anti-trafficking mechanisms, manageable amounts of red tape blocking private enterprise, and investment in their own people, such as in education.

I know this leaves out a majority of poor countries which are unfortunate to have leaders indifferent to these benchmarks. Those citizens are just as deserving as the rest, but MCC is based on the principle that development *can* be done when these conditions are met, and *cannot* be done when not. I, too, would love to find ways of ousting the tight-gripped dinosaurs who deny these mechanisms to their people, but so far there hasn't been a tried and true way of getting rid of them. In the interim, why not reward the few decent ones with trust and resources?

MCC compacts are arduously-negotiated agreements with equal input from recipient and donor. They tend to come in tranches of $350 million, and are rarely repeated after their five-year cycles run out. In the case of Benin, President Yayi's personal commitment to the process, and to the benchmarks that frame the rules and regs protocol, yielded a great gift to his country. Others could do likewise.

Benin is not free of corruption. The 2007 poisoning plot against the president could well have been the work of Monsieur Patrice Talon, former business associate of the president, and likely spurned partner in a bribery scheme. Having someone trying to kill you can get your attention. No proof, but Yayi has carried on and seems to have put his life on the line to get corruption in his country under control. This is news.

You won't see it in many newspapers and blog sites, because (in the slang of journalistic parlance) this was the airplane that took off. Only the ones that crash make it to the front pages. Still, while the task is something like two per cent complete, let us celebrate a rare victory in economic growth through democracy (Benin is growing at six per cent despite having no natural resources) and give a bit of love to those few who say they'll play by the rules, and then actually do so.

Revenge of the Clowns

September 13, 2015

April 11 of this year, as officials from Cuba and the United States of America negotiated a regularization of diplomatic ties after a 50-year hiatus, a U.S. government reporter was ejected from a press conference in Havana. In case you were on Pluto at the time, the United States later opened its embassy in Havana August 14, with Secretary of State John Kerry present.

About the ejected reporter April 11: I'm not sure how this differs from Donald Trump's bodyguards ejecting journalists from Trump rallies, except that Trump is not yet a government, and Cuba is.

Hard feelings all around: when Karen Caballero and her cameraman Rudy Hernandez were barred from the Havana press conference, Carlos García Pérez said, "The fact that Karen and Rudy were forced out of the press conference is further indication of the ongoing lack of press freedom in Cuba." Pérez is director of the Office of Cuba Broadcasting (OCB), which includes Radio and TV Martí.

The Cuban government's resentment of Caballero's employer is understandable if a bit huffy. After 30 years of beaming anti-Castro broadcasts toward "La Isla" (Cuba), U.S. government-funded Radio and TV Martí has a pretty pathetic record. Created in 1985 as an alternative news source for beleaguered Cubans, Martí never reached more than two per cent of the Cuban people, and 90 per cent of Cubans never even knew it existed. Effective jamming by the Cuban government scrambled the signal almost all the time, even and especially during the brave days of broadcasting from a blimp over the Caribbean.

Affectionately known as "Fat Albert," the blimp succumbed to hurricane season in 2005, losing its helium in July 9 and falling down over the Florida Keys. This misfortune did not discourage Radio TV Martí employees from producing lots more helium for their never-heard broadcasts. The ten per cent of Cubans who even knew the broadcasts existed called them *"No se ve TV"* (No-see-TV). The International Telecommunications Union (ITU) has long claimed that the Martís violate international law in taking frequencies not assigned to them by the international body empowered to do so.

The U.S. Government Accountability Office (GAO) also accuses the station of "engaging in political propaganda in the forms of editorializing, use of offensive and incendiary language in broadcasts, use of unsubstantiated reports coming from Cuba, and presentation of individual views as news."

Who provided the helium for all this? The Broadcasting Board of Governors, the bipartisan federal agency of nine, which makes sure radio and TV broadcasters paid by the U.S. government toe the government line and never forget who pays their salaries. One of the nine was a subcontractor of the Department of Defense, paid to remove the Smith-Mundt laws prohibiting the broadcasting of U.S. government propaganda inside the United States. He succeeded in this mission, with Smith-Mundt defanged ("modernized") in 2012.

These measures are supported by Cro-Magnons, elected representatives, who would sabotage nonproliferation agreements, but who cannot even pronounce the word "nuclear."

Propaganda is nasty stuff, whether it is my propaganda, or yours, or somebody else's. Let's try out this definition: a mixture of truth and non-truth, intended to persuade someone of something, while camouflaging the source of the information. Work for you? If so, the Martís would be pretty good examples, and a lethal blow to U.S. credibility for anyone unlikely enough to tune into this blather. Martí is independent to the listener, but purist in its highly-controlled messaging, which by the way has cost the U.S. taxpayer seven hundred million dollars since its inception.

Who is this "U.S. taxpayer," and how can we get a rebate or reparations back to this luckless sot?

If you have sympathy for the Martís' frustrated informationists (in fact I do, and I'm glad there is an employer of last resort for them), take heart: their revenge is imminent. August 27 they posted an RFQ (Request for Quotes) to offer money for anyone who can come up with "uniquely funny, ironic, satirical and entertaining comedy shows targeting Cuban officials, politician and others on the island." Be advised: if you have ever served as Spanish-speaking clown at kids' birthday parties, you might qualify.

You think I'm making this up? Kindly consult BBG50-Q-15-826-OCBSatire on the federal grants website. If you have a SAM and a NAICS and a DUNS number and a NCAGE in your proposal, it will go to the top of the pile. Please limit your RFQ response to six pages, plus a two-page curriculum vitae plus three pages of your track record in producing political satire.

Uncle Sam needs you, and will greatly reward. Note that CLINs must be in USD in English, and your SOW must reflect your successful history in the field. Your final video product must be in DV25 or DVCAM format, and be pursuant to the U.S. FAR.

If you still doubt me, here's the link:

https://www.fbo.gov/index?s=opportunity&mode=form&id=2b52c0eb4ee6c9e48bc1d5dac3f52f5e&tab=core&_cview=0

But hurry, the deadline for submissions is September 14. Questions? Call BBG reps Malita Dyson at (202) 382-7204 or Herman

Shaw, (202) 382-7856.

Oh, and Radio TV Martí has its own internal media censorship and forbids its own employees from asking questions at White House press conferences. Annette López-Muñoz, a Martí employee, broke this unwritten rule November 22, 1986, and was removed from service. She heard she would be offered a job as copy editor but indicated that it was doubtful she would accept it. But that would have been during the Cold War.

An Appreciation of Pat Nixon

October 13, 2015

Now we learn that the reclusive and vile Richard Nixon was even worse than we thought. This thanks to recent revelations by the now 89-year-old Alexander Butterfield, the one who revealed the existence of the White House Tapes which brought Nixon down August 9, 1974.

After three years of raining bombs uselessly over North Vietnam, Nixon knew the indiscriminate killings served no purpose ("zilch" from a memo now disclosed in yet another new book by Bob Woodward).

January 2, 1972, Nixon said in a CBS interview with Dan Rather that the bombing had been "very, very effective." But the "zilch" memo, the more accurate appraisal, was written to Henry Kissinger the day after. I guess this would close the case on Richard Nixon – not as a self-delusional strategist, but as a liar willing to kill hundreds of thousands for the sole purpose of being reelected. In this, he succeeded in late 1972. We who lived through those times knew this to be true, but lacked the smoking gun recently revealed. The new "proof" changes little, except to relegate the President to his private hell for an extended sentence of twice infinity, or however it works in karmic repayments.

A moment of acknowledgement – please! – for his decent and dignified wife, Patricia. Pat Nixon, stuck in the hell of public attachment to this American monster, carried herself with style and candor throughout. We now know that Pat Nixon trailed along her repellent husband even while discreetly maintaining separate living arrangements at the "Winter White House" in Key Biscayne. One day we may learn why she put up with this – I would guess, for reasons of honor and for wishing not to become, herself, an element in American political life. And also from old-fashioned acceptance, with dignity, of a miserable personal fate. There is much to be said in favor of her, holding to values which were consistent then, even if not those we might look for today in a different social context.

Watergate was a rare moment of heroism for an otherwise supine press in the United States – remarkable then, almost non-existent now. Notice how journalists cling to the Watergate example as evidence of their virtues, when there is little else they can point to.

Plenty of them shoved microphones into Pat Nixon's face at the time, hoping for some self-incrimination – or at least some distancing from her largely-estranged husband. No go. Disappointing the vultures consistently, she issued only one comment, and repeatedly: "I know the truth, and soon you will too." How elegant and graceful, how truthful in the midst of a cesspool of Administration lies and a press that saw the whole episode as carrion to feed on.

My own recollection is of the 100th anniversary of Yellowstone National Park, which endeared Pat Nixon forever to me.

Visitors had been brought from sixty countries to "celebrate" the occasion of the founding of our great National Parks movement. Yellowstone was inaugurated in1872 by President Grant, and the 100th was coming up in 1972, the same year as the breaking of the

Watergate drama.

Panjandrums were gathered from the Nixon cabinet to speechify at the outdoors site of a campfire around which explorers and campers came up with the idea of a national park, sometime in 1871. The international visitors were herded onto buses from a hotel to the outdoors site, all unequipped for the freezing sleet of that September afternoon. All had been told at U.S. embassies abroad, "September, an ideal time for tourism in the United States. Moderate temperatures and lovely Indian summer weather." All embassies were clueless about the microclimate in Yellowstone Park, which turned very adverse on a moment's notice in September because of its high elevation. They came in short sleeves and khaki pants.

National park directors from Sri Lanka, Madagascar, Thailand, and four dozen other countries were placed at a park site under a heavy freezing hail with no building in the area, no protection, and no vehicles to allow them to depart the miserable punishment of the afternoon.

Nixon's Secretary of the Interior, Roger C.B. Morton, and other windbags gave endless discourses from under the protective dais covering only them. The hundreds in the audience suffered under the heavy sleet, caught the mother of all flus and colds, silently vowing never to return to such an inhospitable country. The visitors and their camp followers (like me, as interpreter for one of them) began to feel like hostages and sought in vain for a way out of the ordeal. *Kein Außgang.* It seemed the world had gone mad, certainly the Nixon cabinet.

Then Pat Nixon took the microphone, and inserted the sole bit of sanity into an otherwise catastrophic event. She said, "I am so glad to see all of you, and my husband sends his warmest greetings. You may now board the buses to return to your hotel."

I loved Pat Nixon at that moment, and have admired her in retrospect ever since. Very bad circumstances, very high level of dignity and sanity. Poor Pat, to be married to such an ogre. But she made up for her Great Mistake many times over, turning sordid dramas into exemplary behavior for which she has never been properly recognized or thanked.

If karma exists, Little Richard twists and turns in an agony of burning flesh, payback for what he brought upon hundreds of thousands of Southeast Asians, Chileans, guileless American GIs, Bangladeshis and others. Pat, by contrast, maintains a modest, separate residence in Nowhere Land, tending a tiny cottage garden and turning down temporary offers of free digital access to unseemly current events.

The Man No One Would Be
January 5, 2016

Consider the dramatic fate of François Darlan. He was Vichy's likely successor to the reviled Marshal Pétain and heir to France's naval tradition owing to the death of a great-grandfather at the Battle of Trafalgar in 1805. Whence Darlan's loathing of the British (The French live by memory; the British, by method and process; Americans, by outcome. None is correct. All are valid).

Darlan, born in 1881, fell in with the Bad Boys of Vichy in 1940 after Germany's breathtaking destruction of Europe's supposedly grandest army. From the comfortable distance of time, we shouldn't judge whether the Vichy government was inspired more by supine concession, strategic accommodation, timely opportunism, or affinity to the Nazi cause. Only arrogance could lead us to think we might know what went through Frenchmen's heads at this moment of their humiliation. France, mainly, had insisted on the punitive measures at the 1921 Versailles Treaty, fueling Nazi resentment and serving as a factor in their takeover of 1933.

Darlan was made French Admiral Chief of Staff and led the French Navy from 1937, a time of extreme bad luck for anyone who thought Germany might not be a master race.

Darlan's antipathy for the British was only validated when British forces scuttled the French fleet in Toulon during the 1940 debacle. Darlan hated the possibility of French naval vessels falling into the hands of Nazis, but was enraged when the British sank the fleet after correctly seeing his unwillingness to do so himself. He had said to Churchill shortly before France's surrender to the Nazis, "No French ship will ever come into the hands of the Germans." He meant this, and in the long run lived to implement the idea to the best of his limited abilities.

Quite a pickle: concede to German aggression against his country, or reverse a vendetta against the British who had overcome his great-grandfather's Napoleonic ambitions a century and a half earlier? In good French fashion he kept all options alive, with bitterness as the driving force. *Gloire* delayed, *gloire* denied. For the record, I am a Francophile, though I see so-called leader of most nations, at most times, a pestilence.

Admiral Darlan was heir-apparent to the hated Pétain, as the latter aged during the catastrophes of World War II. We will never know if he considered this an honor or a cruel obligation. He had no good options. In May of 1941, he was sent to meet Hitler and Ribbentrop, and approved French concessions to the Nazi program.

Things changed in November of 1942, as American British troops took Tobruk and al-Alamein in North Africa after hideously violent battles "destroying" tens of thousands of troops on both sides.

A little coincidence: Darlan's son was gravely ill in Algiers the day the Allies took the city, and he made a visit to see his son in the hospital. This made him conveniently available for capture by Allies on November 8. He surrendered all French forces under his command November 11, and was given the unenviable task of ordering all the French in Northwest Africa to comply with Allied directives. No playmate for Darlan! Neither French, nor Allied, nor German sympathies for him.

American and British public opinion were outraged that the Allies would give governing authority to a Vichy leader. Churchill argues that in the middle of a war, the Russian maxim applied: "Walk with the Devil as far as the other side of the bridge."

Darlan would not have been a first pick for anyone's basketball team, shirts or skins. This was a man no one wanted, his goose cooked, his bad made by being "on the wrong side of history" and then some. How is a well-meaning patriot to know?

Christmas Eve, 1942, Darlan was assassinated by a French monarchist opposed to Vichy. All were relieved. What was one to do with such a moral and political leper? Assassin Fernand Bonnier de La Chapelle was executed for the deed by firing squad, December 26, 1942. Dramatization coming to a multiplex near you, opening date unknown.

Some have accused Churchill of engineering the assassination for the convenience of the Alliance. I think not. In some of the more contemplative passages in Churchill's War Diaries, he says:

> Few men have paid more heavily for errors of judgment and failure of character… In accordance with his repeated promises, he ought in 1940 to have ordered the fleets to Britain, to the U.S., the African posts, anywhere out of German power. Then, perhaps influenced by motive of a department character, he gave his allegiance to Marshal Pétain's government… Ambition stimulated his errors.
> …For a year and a half he had been a great power in shattered France. At the time when we descended upon North Africa he was undoubted heir of the aging Marshal. Now suddenly a cataract of amazing events fell upon him… He brought to the Anglo-American allies exactly what they needed, namely, a French voice, which all French officers and officials in this vast theater, now plunged in the war, would obey. He struck his final blow for us, and it is not for those who benefited enormously from his accession to our side to revile his memory… It seemed obvious at the time that he was wrong in not sailing the French fleet to allied or neutral ports in June 1940; but he was right in his second fearful decisions. …Always he had declared [the Toulon

fleet] would never fall into German hands. In this undertaking before history he did not fail. Let him rest in peace, and let us all be thankful we have never had to face the trials under which he broke.

[*Hinge of Fate*, Volume 4, 1951]

A Cure Worse Than the Disease

January 10, 2016

In their persuasive op/ed of January 5, two great public servants argue for more beef in countering Putin, ISIS, and other propaganda mills working against us. Paula Dobriansky, a clear-throated advocate for freedom of expression and transparency under the George W. Bush administration, and David Rivkin, who ably served in the Justice Department and the White House under Presidents Reagan and George H.W. Bush, bring this up as a matter for urgent policy attention. In this, they are right.

Their *cri de coeur* is most timely, and reminds us that the Cold War never really went away; it just staged remakes with different actors. The world remains dangerous, and vigilance needs to be more energetic than ever.

The problem is, as medicine, House Bill 2323, now under consideration to revamp U.S. government broadcasting, is worse than the disease. It should be plucked in its infancy and sent back for rehab.

As Dobriansky and Rivkin correctly remind us, even Secretary of State Hillary Clinton said in Senate hearings in 2013, "[The U.S. Government Board of Broadcasting Governors] is practically a defunct agency in terms of its capacity to be able to tell a message around the world. So we're abdicating the ideological arena and need to get back into it."

The BBG is a clunky entity, staffed by part-timers, and fails to coordinate the sprawling world of radio, television, social messaging, web links and rest, which bring accurate news in 47 languages to all continents. It happens to have an able, dedicated CEO only as of September 14, 2015, when John Lansing moved into the position which has served as target practice for frustrated communicators and reorganizers.

Given adequate authority, Lansing and his successors will be well able to advance the cause of more effective U.S. government broadcasting. Creating yet new layers of bureaucracy will not.

The Voice of America, created in 1942 to counter Nazi propaganda, still serves the interest of unbiased information, and on this basis has earned a universal reputation for accurate sourcing in a world crowded with private, national, and commercial networks with axes to grind.

The firewall between it and the U.S. government (sneered at by skeptics but nevertheless solid to date) has rendered record listenership based on its credibility. While American skeptics often doubt it, VOA has a universal standard of veracity which at times has pitted it against the ephemeral actions of its funders. Listeners overseas know this, and tune in with increasing numbers. While the "surrogate" broadcasters—Radio Free Europe, Radio Liberty, Radio Martí, and others—carry on courageously, their signals are easily scrambled by hostile regimes where VOA manages to get through – and currently has a non-negligible audience of two million inside Russia.

For $749 million a year, U.S. government broadcasting gets a proven 226 million listeners per week. Proven "hits" count more than "potential listeners," which is the standard for RT and CCTV impact ("Seven hundred million!" says RT).

House Bill 2323 calls for new layers of "coordination" which would muddy the already confusing overlays of authorities and would pit one U.S. government broadcaster against the other in vying for scarce operating funds. The objective should be to reduce the layers to more coherence, not create yet new confusion. A double-headed monster we do not need.

Most ludicrously, it would create an "International Communications Agency" – stop the presses! This was the same silly mistake made by Jimmy Carter in the 1970s, when he word-smithed himself into this dead-end phrase, the acronym easily confused with an agency which does not promote transparency. I well remember the warm welcome we received in 1978 when I checked into a hotel in New Orleans with five official African visitors, the hostess beaming, "Welcome to our delegation from the CIA!" Americans supposedly do not repeat mistakes as stupid as this one.

The good news is, talk of obliging the VOA to report on news in the United States only, with U.S. policy as an overlay, was correctly set aside in the drafting of the bill. This gaffe, from last year's bill 4490, would have killed our audiences forever, everywhere. How best to counter crude propaganda: create yet more crude propaganda ourselves? Clearly not, and we've dodged that bullet just for the moment. Rue the day it might ever return.

But the text still carries a ton of lint and threatens both the independence and the coherence of our octopus broadcasters. Yes, different broadcasters under the same funder should avoid duplication and coordinate roles, but this is not done with a wave of the wand or a paragraph in a bill. It happens in the newsrooms and open discussions among the able employees of the broadcasters.

China spends seven billion dollars per year on international broadcasting, with scant results and not much trust from its potential listeners. With $749 million for all its facets, the VOA and "surrogates" have earned and kept vast audiences in Africa, Latin America, the Middle East, Asia, and the "two" Europes. People still want information, and they are perfectly capable of knowing when their local broadcasters in repressive countries do not supply it.

Kindly double or treble its funding. If you think we should have adequate answers to Putin and other propaganda, don't fiddle with an already sprawling structure to make it more unwieldy. Heaven forfend that the Senate should ever come up with a draft as flawed as House Bill 2323.

Keeping the Memory
January 25, 2016

If memory civilizes us, forgetting is how we unattain what we have attained.

January 15, scholars gathered at the Wilson Center's Kennan Institute to honor the outgoing Librarian of Congress, James Billington. Washington's gossip press gave Billington a hard time in 2015, nailing him as just not cool and with the times, in digitizing this immense repository of human culture as quickly as he might have. Never mind that he foresaw the digitization process and raced to convert millions of LoC documents to less perishable form – while also championing ways to avoid printing on acid-based paper, which guarantees the timed destruction of written documents.

Of the individuals gathered, Ismail Serageldin gets special mention. For the occasion, he traveled from Alexandria (the one in Egypt) to reflect on the successes of his friend Billington and on the so-far undying concept of world culture. This concept can always wither in barbaric times.

The original Library of Alexandria, named after "The Great," housed the largest collection of books and scrolls in ancient times.

The site held mythic presence even during the 1600 years since its destruction in 391. Or we could say, after its partial destruction in 48 BCE, when Caesar's troops scuttled their own ships in their fight against Egyptian Pharaoh Ptolemy XIII. Three centuries before Caesar, Alexander had a reputable tutor, one Aristotle. Knowledge was power then, and apparently still is.

With digitization and other crazy and almost daily technological advances in information sharing, libraries become exponentially more valuable, not less. The process is in full bloom of course, but on the use and application of more information for more people than ever, the jury is still out. As Mark Twain said when telecommunications crossed North America, "Maine can now talk to California, but Maine has nothing to say."

Having the primary sources in captivity is a good start, but means nothing until they are put to use. "Information – to intelligence – to wisdom." This is the challenge, still. All the toys in the world, but spotty application to lift humans to where they might be.

Ismail Serageldin had a good gig 1992-2000 as vice president of the World Bank.

January 15 he told me it was a no-brainer to leave that position and take up the challenge of recreating the Alexandria Library for modern times, now slightly renamed the Bibliotheca Alexandrina (the BA) inaugurated with magnificent new digs in 2002.

The DC discussion January 15 was a treasure in itself, with four soaring intellects reminding us that Billington's function as an historian is no less significant than his abilities to bring America's memory bank to modernity. One of the discussants, James F. Collins, U.S. Ambassador to Moscow during the happily failed coup attempt of August 1991, said that in seeking best actions as a diplomat during times of crisis, he would always consult historians first, political scientists and bureaucrats later. His teacher on Russian history, 48 years earlier, was one James Billington (author, among other works, of *The Icon and the Axe*).

Another, Armenian-born Vartan Gregorian (former director, New York Public Library and president, Brown University), said that the United States has no ministry of culture, but has the Library of Congress instead.

The Wilson Center seems to have taken down the 90-minute video of this once-only discussion, also including Serageldin, Gregorian, Collins, and also Blair Ruble, former director of the Kennan Institute.

I append the link, just in case the video is ever put back up. Don't miss viewing it, if it is:

https://www.wilsoncenter.org/event/celebrating-james-billington-the-librarian-congress-emeritus-lifetime-advancing-knowledge-the

Libraries—*the* Library—have a different but more powerful meaning today than ever. A library becomes less a place, more a unifying concept. The American Memory program in LoC, created by Billington, records oral histories and reflects our antecedents, helping to make us see ourselves in context. In the visual arts, the equivalent would be 3-D depictions. Memory, as all four discussants said in four different ways, is not national, but the possession of humans. Especially now, with internet access reaching nearly everyone.

African twentieth-century scholar Amadou Hampâté Bâ once said, "When an old man dies, it is a library burning."

This sounds like a sermon, and is not meant to be. The excitement in the room that Friday was tactile, and should belong to all. I hope the Wilson Center puts the video back up, so we can recover the words, otherwise lost, of a remarkable tribute and encomium not only for a man, but for the preservation of memories through whatever form.

Libraries like the BA can no longer be burned as before, now that they are also on clouds. Processing is another matter. Drinking from a fire hose has its challenges, and will still require the Aristotles, individuals with brains on fire, to make meaning of it all.

Haiti's Amazing Language

January 25, 2016

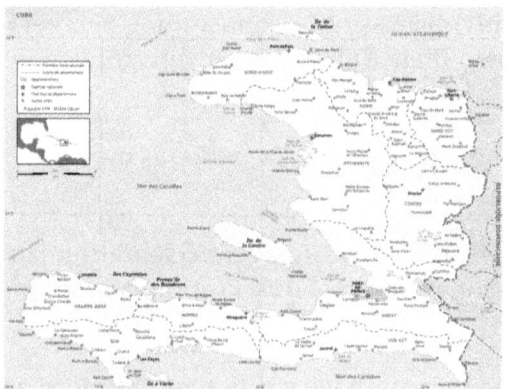

Today's news shows us a new political crisis in Haiti, the country that least needs yet another. Guy Philippe, Senatorial candidate for a governmental body that went into deep freeze a year ago, calls for a popular uprising if current president Michel Martelly is kicked out of office at the end of his term, February 7. Martelly was supposed to hold elections by the second Monday of 2015, to replace the not-sitting Senate. He finally did so months late, and the new Senate is in place as of January 12, 2016, albeit with some seats still undecided. He has been ruling by decree for the better part of the year in between.

This would be the same Guy Philippe who overthrew the Aristide regime February 28, 2014. Something fishy here: Philippe's little brigade of 200 troops came in with neatly pressed uniforms and state-of-the-art weapons after months of scrupulous training in neighboring Dominican Republic. DR has no secrets, but somehow provided the real estate and freedom of movement for the only disciplined troops Haiti has had in over a century. Philippe's band came over the border to cheering townspeople along the way, and up to the capital of Port-au-Prince. They would have killed Aristide if the United States had not rescued the latter in a small plane provided by U.S. military.

Philippe has now reversed his earlier function, rallying citizens behind a national leader instead of seeking to kill him. Things happen, people evolve.

If this seems confusing, understand that Haitians understand every iota of the illogical world they live in. Outsiders never will.

It is inherent in their language, so grammatically simple, so confounding to those not born into it.

For years, the only text for learning the Haitian Creole language (encouraged by Jean-Claude "Baby Doc" Duvalier and enshrined in the 1987 Constitution after his departure) was *Ann Pale Kreyòl*. This playful text was published by the University of Indiana in 1988 for English speakers.

In it we learn that *"Li li li pou li"* can mean "She reads it to him," or "She reads him to him," or "He reads it to him," and so forth – basically anything you want. This can seem ambiguous to the learner, but Haitian are never been misled, they always know the context.

Ann Pale Kreyòl gives us life the way it really is in catastrophic, gorgeous, seductive Haiti. Lesson eight gives us standard dialogues like *"Ki sa l'ap fè?"* ("What is he doing?") Then the answer: *"L'ap plante."* ("He's planting.")

As the text progresses, we get slightly more complex situations: *"Tidjo gen yon liv nan men li."* ("Little Joe holds a book in his hands.")

But in the advanced chapters, we get to the nitty-gritty: Lamèsi ("Thanks-to-God") learns that her daughter has died in the capital and is going to get the body to bury her back home near Jérémie. Her brother says *"Adye o! M fèk pran nouvèl la, wi. Ki sa ou ap fè? W'ap pran batiman pou'w al Pòtoprens?"* ("Oh my God, I just learned the news! What are you going to do? You're going to take your boat to Port-au-Prince?")

This quickly becomes a language lesson in modes of transport – *"batiman"* (boat), *"kamyon"* (truck), *"chwal"* (horse). But the text masterfully gives the real-life situations one would run into in the ill-fated isle: premature death, family solidarity, and grieving. This is a text that does not mince words, and which goes into the real context of everyday life.

As we advance, things get worse, and murder comes into focus: *Veye a komanse; men bri kouri li pa mouri bon mò. Y'ap pale pou yo wè kijan oungan an ap ranje li pou moun ki touye'l la ka peye konsekans zak li.* ("The wake has started, but it is rumored that she didn't die naturally. They're talking to see how the *oungan* [vodou priest] will prepare the corpse so that the person who killed her can pay for her action.")

The final dialogue in the Indiana text goes like this:

Kote moun yo? Nou pare pou mwen? ("Where is everybody? Are you ready for me?)

Wi papa! Tout bagay pare, wi. Mò a nan ti chanm nan. ("Yes, Dad! Everything is ready! The dead person is in the little room.")

And we even learn the motive for the murder, that "It's a light skinned woman with long hair who killed her because Pierre married her." (*Se yon fi wouj gwo cheve ki touye'l paske Pye marye ak li.*)

Here is a text that soars above banality and depicts the harsh realities of Haitian everyday life.

Getting back to Guy Philippe and the current crisis of the day: When Aristide was taken away February 28, 2004, the airplane pilot turned to his passenger and said, "Where to?"

"Ban'm Guy!" said Aristide, sputtering with rage: literally, "Give me Guy!" or, more liberally translated, "Get me Guy Philippe's head on a pike!"

The pilot heard only *"Ban'm Guy"* and set the navigational system on Bangui, the capital of Central African Republic, where Aristide ended up three days later.

The Center Folds

February 19, 2016

Remember Mike McCurry? During the Lewinsky scandal, he had about the most difficult job in human history: spokesman for the Clinton White House ("Mommy, what's a 'blow job'?").

McCurry did a masterful job, remained gracious, truthful, and responsive throughout. He never dodged a question, never sought to deceive. Preceded by Dee Dee Myers, he stayed at the helm from 1995 to 1998. Mike was in a rock-hard-place at the time, and was adored by many in the press corps who appreciated his forthcoming interactions.

People might forget that he was also State Department spokesman before that, 1993-95, under SecState Warren Christopher.

February 17 he spoke with diplomats at a Washington club and was fully in his element. Taking head-on the zaniness of the current electoral process, he lamented the disappearance of the "Center," which traditionally has been the leavening of American political life. Of course the Center has now disappeared. It may one day be restored, but not in the imaginable future. Everybody knows that.

McCurry is a specialist in working for losing candidates, having backed Bruce Babbit, Bob Kerrey, Lloyd Bentsen, and John Kerry for presidential and vice presidential bids. Evidently both Democratic candidates have begged him these days to keep his distance lest he jinx them.

Now a professor at the Wesley Theological Seminary, McCurry has landed on the eroding banks of a swiftly-flowing rapids.

His message February 17 was a powerful one: foreign policy rhetoric during presidential campaigns tends to be the contrary of implementation once a candidate wins in the ordeal of an American election. When campaigning in 1998, Bill Clinton focused on Haiti, Somalia, and Bosnia, laying down a "muscular" marker to distinguish himself from feckless actions of his predecessor in the White House. Once called on actually to do something about these three issues, he left a trail of broken promises and disappointments.

The inverse in 2016 gives us perverse hope: as no one in the so-called presidential campaign (I mean No One) has any opinion about the United States' place in the world, the likelihood is that whoever is elected may actually come up with a foreign policy.

This is not an entirely snarky notion. Saying nothing in the campaigns, candidates in presidential campaigns tend to spout the opposite of what they actually do later when (shudder) they are elected. Following this logic, saying nothing at this point in the campaign might actually yield some results after the slugfest is over in November.

McCurry was possibly grasping for straws here in his comments, but the logic followed.

This observation has a certain pathos, as the world withdraws in horror at the spectacle of our current political debates. Candidates mention in passing Mexico, Iraq, China, Russia, and Syria (maybe Iran and Cuba), but that's about all. Ahem, there are nearly 200 countries in the world, and apparently 193 of them are not worthy of thought or comment. Even a former secretary of state talks only of Libya, and then only under duress. The world does not exist – peek-a-boo! If I cover my eyes, it goes away. So-called foreign policy debates have to do with cached emails, security lapses at a single consulate, and punishment of the few we really do not like. Never mind major trade treaties now up for ratification, which could profoundly affect our GNP and levels of employment, or the development of rapidly-growing economies which one day soon will constitute our export markets. Never mind the dictatorships and presidents-for-life in countries which could be our partners in so many ways.

McCurry notes the bizarre irony that one of our candidates' knowledge of foreign policy makes a "net negative" in the campaign. This is a new form of isolationism we haven't seen even in the darkest days of our sleeping dinosaur's anxiety dreams.

Indeed, the Center does not hold. The Center was long the hope for a recognizable America, and a way of measuring our many dependents' need for us to be predictable.

The media, which used to be the "referee" in American political mud fights, is now a highly fickle cheering squad.

McCurry, in addition to his new life as a professor of Methodist theology, also serves on the Commission on Presidential Debates. The Commission is not a mandated body, but serves to regulate the tone and content of the post-nomination debates: traditionally one domestic, one foreign, one a town hall. It seems this is now being rethought, since these themes no long interest the American voter. As the dominant underlying factor in our national consciousness, despair needs to be the subject of public discussions so as to muster a viewing audience. Compare the Americans' despair to that of the average Zimbabwean or Brazilian, and the level of bizarreries exponentially increases by our incredulous followers in other countries. Those who have for so long relied on us now must find their own way, since the Master has gone blind and mad. Maybe it is just as well, since we were never up to this leadership thing in the first place.

One can only sigh, lament, and carry on. In the meantime, Michael

McCurry does sure-footed imitations of Lyndon Johnson, Bill Clinton, and the great Daniel Patrick Moynihan. Even for this alone, he must be greatly admired.

And—word from the oracle—"The one very predictable factor is that something unpredictable will happen." Step up and affirm, if you have any other way of viewing the currently debauched political discourse.

Old Wine, New Battles
March 1, 2016

The February 28-29 *New York Times* gave us more than we previously knew about the Obama White House's 2011 decision to go in with French and UK in bombing Libya. If the fact-checkers are correct, our eyes have reason to pop out of our heads. Authors Jo Becker and Scott Shane document the heated moment, signaling that within the Administration, good brains got together but went for a poison pill. It appears the secretary of state drew the team in the direction of targeted bombing. This was no easy decision, and good discussions came out on both sides.

The prevailing argument was the United Nations' recently unveiled practice of "R2P," "Responsibility to Protect." Civilian populations, after all, were under direct and explicit threats from a madman, Muammar Khadafi.

Then-Secretary of Defense Robert Gates called this "The 51-49 Decision," with Secretary Clinton casting the swing vote.

This was not a strategic or moral failure, just the best guess under stressful conditions. Unfortunately, it drew U.S. foreign policy once again into a cul-de-sac of unintended consequences, aka "Mission Creep." Libya went to hell (might have done so in any case) and now is a threat to itself, to Europe, and even to U.S. security interests with its new status as a playground and R&R stop for terrorists.

No political party in America is immune to myopic actions which create more problems than they solve. Democratic and Republican administrations both used deceit and ill-aimed firepower in prosecuting a Vietnam War that had no hope of a useful outcome. Our political parties have led us to lose-lose outcomes, harming many and helping few. The paradigms and "table-top exercises" never worked, and still don't. America—the nation of pragmatism— needs new models, not to avoid the responsibilities of being superpower, but to employ them to successful outcomes.

In the lead-up to the George W. Bush Administration's disastrous invasion of Iraq in March 2003, White House cronies were suckered by the late Ahmed Chalabi, who gave neo-cons the shoddy narrative they craved, inveigling American force to work a regime change which led only from tragedy to greater tragedy. American credibility in the Arab world and elsewhere suffered blows which may take a generation or more to overcome, if ever. American political parties have a pretty bad record of taking the first charlatan who comes along and pitting its might to the whims of manipulative Rasputins.

Likewise, in spring of 2011, according to Becker and Shane, Libyan smooth talker Mahmoud Jibril (later the prime minister du jour) convinced the secretary of state in a hotel room in Paris to put her considerable weight into an ill-fated intervention in Libya. We were duped into a group military action with France and the United Kingdom, which led to two months of hostilities in the North African nation, then under the heels of a perverted dictator, now engulfed in a chaos with no apparent end. The action violated the War Powers Act by a few days, then got lucky as Khadafi was pulled out of a cement tunnel by enraged rebels, sodomized by a bayonet and then killed. The point of the 1973 War Powers Act was to condition undeclared wars on Congressional approval after 60 days. There was a big "What if" tied to the Libya action had it gone much beyond the 60-day limit.

The motivation for the Libya intervention was laudable. The flaw was the failure to consider fully the outcome. Anyone can make mistakes, but those who lead us and innocent populations to distress should be held to account for their miscalculations, especially when they seek continued authority to do so.

The Senate's approval of George W. Bush's war in Iraq was not unique to any individual or party. "The Record" is and should be an unforgiving mirror to the successes and failures of America's decision makers – in this instance, the Senate. Individuals making misjudgments may be seen favorably for their motives, but mistakes and miscalculations get the full light of the sun in a democracy and system of accountability.

We are not talking here about the banalities of "hawkishness" and "dovishness," since each circumstance is unique. Saying that a superpower can or should abdicate its role in the world is too facile a generalization. But nor can one country, no matter how powerful, solve the problems of all with short-term actions. The art and science of policy is to make the best judgment possible with the information given at a particular juncture of crisis.

Engaging in the Libya conflict in 2011 (without any plan for an outcome) was not morally or even tactically "wrong." However, events have gone against American interests – and also, by the way, the beleaguered populations of the current Libya, which is a threat to itself, to Europe, and sooner or later to American direct security interests as well.

Good people can make bad decisions, and the Libya caper unfortunately was a bad one. French President Sarkozy and British Prime Minister Blair got the Obama White House into a military action in Libya which indeed unseated Muammar Khadafi, but which alas did no good for the region or for attempts to restrain chaos and terrorism, both of which run rife in Libya today.

National Security Advisor Susan Rice opposed the action, but was outmaneuvered by Secretary Clinton. Both were sincere in their convictions, both armed with solid arguments. One had to be right in the outcome, the other wrong.

Infallibility and omniscience are not offered to policy leaders in times of crisis. Colin Powell said plainly enough, engage in conflict only with an exit plan and with overwhelming force. Better, of course, not to enter conflict at all if it is avoidable. The records of both political parties in America have misled us too often, and have taken us to perilous scenarios unwittingly betraying our national values. Experience is not wisdom. We need greater thought, with the nuance both parties have failed to display, as we enter twenty-first century challenges.

You Say Boots, I Say Rubbers

April 11, 2016

Freezing rain in an English village. My shoes were soaked. I ducked into the local pharmacy (Boots) to see if they might have something that could keep my shoes dry. "Boots" is to England what "CVS" is to the United States. I knew that.

I pointed at my wet shoes and said, "I need rubbers, or something." The clerk cast a kindly look and said, "Do you mean 'boots'?"

I knew the word "overshoes," but couldn't remember it at that moment.

"Not boots exactly, just something to keep my feet dry," I said. I figured that ought to explain all I needed on that rainy day.

"Well, this *is* Boots," the clerk answered.

"I know," I said, glancing at the store's logo above.

"So you need rubbers?" the clerk helpfully said.

"I think so, yes."

"Well you'll have to see the pharmacist for that."

"Pharmacist?"

I knew that European pharmacies were a bit more fuddy-duddy than American drug stores, which sold everything from small vacuum cleaners to sophisticated chocolate bars.

"Right," said the clerk.

"I just want something to keep my shoes dry," I said.

"But are you feeling lucky today? Because if so, the pharmacist can best help you."

I said, "I guess I am sort of lucky to be in your charming town, but really I only need some rubbers to keep my shoes dry."

The clerk gave me a conspiratorial and approving glance.

"So you need boots, is that right?" she said.

"Not exactly boots. Just rubbers, or what do you call them…?" I answered.

I knew that "rubbers" were "condoms" in the United States, but didn't think the same slang applied in the United Kingdom. What I didn't realize was that the English equivalent was "boots." I did know about "French letters," but that didn't seem to count.

"We *are* Boots. Evidently you are looking for rubbers. The pharmacist can help."

I realized we were at a cultural and lexical impasse. I saw the item on the shelf, and pointed to it.

"You mean, 'overshoes'?"

"I think that's what I mean."

"If you want just something to keep your shoes dry, it's a bit late now since they are already soaked. Just look at them. What you might have done, earlier today, would have been to fetch some overshoes and get them on in time to deal with this rain we're having."

"You couldn't be more right," I said, reaching for the item on the shelf whose name I no longer sought to know.

"Again," said the clerk, "If you are feeling lucky, the pharmacist can best help."

"I am surely lucky to be in your lovely village," I said. "But I don't expect better luck than that for today. The overshoes will be great, and thanks enormously."

I took the item and managed to get the pair over my soaked shoes, more keeping the water in than out. It was no minor achievement to find rubbers in a Boots. I would have added condoms, but there wouldn't be much use for those on that day.

Luckily, we were all speaking English.

The Old Block

April 14, 2016

While you were distracted by the U.S. election primaries last week, some knives—and also guns—came out in the Republic of Congo (ROC). Eighteen were killed. There, in Brazzaville, one of the Methuselahs of African politics claimed a gazillionth victory in the presidential elections. Denis Sassou Nguesso had first been president in 1979 (the previous century, that is) and stayed in place more or less ever since. He took a leave of absence only in 1992-97, while the country unraveled during a brutal civil war. We who lived in ROC used to call him "Denis Sans-le-Sou," or "Penniless Denis." He came back as de facto transition leader in 2002 after leading the military charge against one rival, Pascal Lissouba, who happened to be president at the time. Then Denis SLS took up his old post of de jure president in 2009.

The ruckus resumed in March-April 2016, when Sassou ran to succeed himself and go into a twentieth year as leader of his diminutive country. Or, if you want to count his in-and-out presence in the national political scene, let's call it 35 years.

Mind you, ROC is a lovely little country with lively and humor-filled individuals who love a joke – unlike the apocalyptic Democratic Republic of the Congo (DRC) across the river. Sassou benefited from Soviet assistance during the Cold War, then from a modest but steady stream of oil revenues in the period following. Nice place to be in charge, and I don't think anyone ever starved in ROC.

This past month some dustups occurred on April 4, as a Jeffersonian opposition group called "The Ninjas" attacked a military post in the capital, killing a half dozen Congolese military and over a dozen civilians caught in harm's way. Amnesty International says that the Ninjas used rape as an instrument of political power, and targeted civilians in its military operations.

The leader of this uprising was election runner-up Guy-Brice Parfait Kolélas, who has since called for peace, and said on April 5, "I accept the Constitutional Court's verdict [giving victory to Denis SLS], however questionable… I nonetheless invite President Sassou Nguesso, the declared winner, to be humble in victory because this election has been marred by all sorts of irregularities."

Nice outcome, but for the civilian and military victims of a contest between the Bad and the Worse. Guy Brice was "Parfait," but in some ways imperfect.

At a youthful 73, Sassou SLS may last another ten, twenty years if he's lucky. Kolélas's party, the MCDDI, is not "One Thousand One Hundred and Twenty-One" as the Roman numerals would suggest, but the Congolese Movement for Democracy and Integral Development.

I knew Kolélas's father, Bernard. He was briefly mayor of ROC's capital, Brazzaville, in the mid-1990s, and even more briefly prime minister of the country during the 1997 civil war. Horatio, I knew him.

Bernard Kolélas was one of the more noble individuals I have met. If he had been born in France, he would have been a Dadaist or at worst, a Surrealist. He spent time in the slammer in 1969-71 for mounting an unsuccessful coup against 1970s president Marien Ngouabi. Later he went back for a prison post-doc, 1978 to 1980. He served as head of something called the National Mediation Committee during the brutal civil war of 1997, then went into exile until being sentenced to death in absentia in 2000. Denis SLS allowed Bernard to attend his wife's funeral in Brazzaville in 2005, then the National Assembly gave him amnesty in 2005. He went a bit gaga and died in Paris in 2009.

I met Kolélas *père* one steamy summer evening in Washington in 1984. He had come with his organizing committee for a run at presidential office, and was looking for moral and financial backing from the rich Outside. The committee consisted of three members – himself and two others, one of whom was Sony La'bou Tansi, the notable Congolese novelist. As political operatives, they were lacking in refinement. In sincerity and singleness of purpose, though, they exceeded others, and certainly any of the current pretenders for the U.S. presidency at this time, April 2016.

They presented their case to me and asked for any support I could muster. I knew I was a Nobody, but they didn't want to take my word for it.

I said, "Well, there is the Socialist International and the Liberal International. So, which one would be your kind of group?" I was thinking of the way Europeans divvy up the world and assist political initiatives in poor countries, as our own National Democratic Institute and International Republican Institute do in our own country.

The delegation of three looked puzzled, and had a brief consultation in Lingala or whatever language they shared and I didn't. I tried to assist: "So are you more or less a left-of-center party, or right-of-center?" This confounded them even more, and led to more Lingala palaver.

After a brief interlude and rapid consensus, Bernard Kolélas said to me, "We don't know if we are right or left. We know only that we are in favor of the full flourishing ["épanouissement"] of the human being."

There they had me. I thought, but perhaps did not say, "I love you, I champion you, I will do anything for you. I am yours, and forever."

The campaign for presidency did not go well, but Koulélas got to be mayor of Brazzaville, which in a Congolese context is not tuna fish.

His little son the Ninja did rile up some street fights and got some innocent people killed last week. But then he got down to business and defused a potential civil war in his country, I would like to think, under the influence of his kindly and harmless father. Vive Kolélas and political ineptitude; it may well be our best hope for a benign future even in our complicated and cumbersome United States.

Late Lunch
May 27, 2016

Spring 1989, and things were about to happen. In Washington, Moscow, Tiananmen Square, Berlin.

Our Assistant Secretary for Europe, Roz Ridgway, was one of the best we ever had. She'd been ambassador to Finland, a country called East Germany, and was running summits between Presidents Reagan and Gorbachev. She would have made a great secretary of state, but people who come up through in the ranks don't get the top jobs.

Our little team was at the periphery of the drama in Madrid. No upheavals there at the time, but it was part of Europe after all, and would have a big Middle East Peace Conference within a couple of years. Something might have come of that, but it wasn't Madrid's fault that it didn't.

We were running our press shop at the U.S. Embassy, riding on cascades of resources finagled by Charles Wick of USIA, as well as Madrid's good fortune of being rid of a dictatorship (1975) and well on its way to catching up with other Western European democracies. Washington pushed resources at us, and we knew better than to question these gifts.

Wick had spawned a clunky communication system, WORLDNET (always spelled out in caps, although they never explained why). It allowed for one-way video on rented satellite time ($10,000 per hour) and gave live interviews for very select audiences overseas. David Brinkley once asked Wick in 1985 on live TV how big the audience was for WORLDNET. Wick said with a straight face, "Two billion," pulling the figure from Mad Hatter's hat.

Brinkley repeated the question a few times, in case he might have misheard the answer. But there it was, and he just went on to the next question. No one ever figured out the real audience for WORLDNET, which was delivered by TV screen to hotel rooms worldwide, something like a *USA Today* equivalent, and taken about as seriously. Skype wasn't even a gleam yet in anyone's eye.

The satellite broadcast times were by reservation, and in the field we couldn't do much about changing them. Spaniards were not obsessed much with ritual in the 1980s, but lunch was serious business, and a nation of forty million went by a schedule developed over the centuries: lunch at 3:00pm, return to the office around 5:00pm, work until 6:00 PM, then home. It seemed strange to Americans, but it was Spain. Only the siesta had fallen by the wayside in a modern and busy city where people could not get home for lunch.

We tried to explain to Washington that the 3:00pm interview time was unwieldy for our local audiences of select journalists, that it would be culturally and logistically impossible to herd them into a studio room at that hour. Our colleagues in Washington thought this was laughable, and a reflection of our laziness. If we were lucky enough to get posted to Madrid, they said, we shouldn't try to rub it in by being offline at 3:00pm, still in the peak of the work day.

We protested in vain.

Unlike the others, our Spanish colleague Natalia León had perfect English and understood our plight. "If you ever find yourself without an audience," she said oh-so-generously, "just use my name." In the broadcasts you could see the speaker in Washington; when the dialogue turned to the field, WORLDNET just projected a still picture of the post involved. For Madrid, I think it was the Plaza Cibeles, with the main post office Correos in the background.

So it came time to talk about what we now know was about to be the end of the Cold War. That day we had Vienna, Budapest, and Madrid on line. It got to be 2:45, 2:50, 2:55 PM… and no one showed up. This was like having *Madame Butterfly* at the Met and missing a soprano. There was stress.

Ridgway gave one of her well-considered opening comments, and the DC producer turned to Vienna for journalists' questions. The two of us in the studio in Madrid needed divine intervention before it got to be our turn. As a backup, we planned to jump dramatically out the nearest window. The first was a shaky plan, and the second wouldn't make much of an impression since we were on the ground floor of the building.

Fifteen minutes into the hour-long program, the production crew in Washington put Madrid on line. Drawing on I don't know what survival instinct, I made up a question myself, and put in a journalist's name. I stated the question for the phantom journalist, making it through by putting on my own voice as the "translator." We got away with it and Ridgway gave a well-crafted answer.

The sweat glowed, however, and somehow we had to survive the next 45 minutes and likely two or three more turns to go on the air. No Spanish journalists in our studio, not even one.

On the third pass I had run out of ammo, and had to use Natalia's name, so as not to misrepresent others. I said, "Question from Natalia León…"

Ridgway interrupted with a big smile and a puff of pleasure: "Natalia! My good friend! Let's hear you in your perfect English. Waiting to hear your voice on the air."

This was what Spaniards call "going from Guatemala to Guatepeor" – the frying pan to the fire.

Now how was I supposed to get myself out of this one, and why hadn't Natalia told us she was a *friend* of Roz Ridgway?

The satellite connection burped at that moment, and there were a couple seconds of static. The Washington producers switched to Vienna and the time ran out before we got another pass.

And thus as the saying goes, "The Angel of Death…" Our misfortunes are masked by others' errors and little acts of God which save us at times. There was a time when these were called "miracles."

All due apologies to the great Roz Ridgway at this late stage. She now sits on a half dozen boards and is thriving in the private sector. Best wishes and admiration to her. Natalia could have been more forthcoming, but her friendship was solid and her intentions benign. We seldom get what we deserve, and seldom get more than we deserve. So thanks anyway for that.

Answer Coming Soon
May 31, 2016

In a *Reuters* story May 29, a disgruntled British journalist talked of PM David Cameron's strategic evasion of media hounds at the 2016 G7 Summit in Japan. The press wanted Cameron's comments on the possible Brexit, but Cameron's team spirited the press away in Ise-Shima to a dance and music show, miles away from where the meetings were. "Lacking stories on the elephant in the room UK media were forced to look for news elsewhere."

It's an old and established tradition. *Fade to June 1987...*

Little waves lapped at the Lido beach, just a quick vaporetto ride from Venice's Piazza San Marco. Too good to be true: barely pre-climate change Venice, only without the claustrophobia and voracious crowds clicking on photo-familiar landmarks in the center of the city. Tranquility. June breezes off the Adriatic, unruffled local restaurants, and time passing lazily.

Seven thousand journalists were descending on Venice for the G7 Summit. All were ready to pounce on the tiny Island of San Giorgio Maggiore in the yawning jaw of the Grand Canal, but few would ever make it to that protected redoubt. There the principals would soon arrive and do much of their real negotiations behind closed doors at the dining room tables away from the glare of the public sessions and briefings. The sixteenth-century Benedictine church had one of the most effective moats in the world: the Grand Canal on every side.

We media aides arrived five days before the meeting, setting up filing centers and eyeballing water routes to the meeting sites. Almost all the vaporettos, and most of the gondolas, had been chartered for the week, since they were the only means for getting from one place to another.

There were the scribes, the photographers, a few video people back then. We few drones on the government side braced for the media crush, wanting to please the 7,000 wherever we could. The pickings would be slim, though.

My boss at the time, the Dumbest Man Ever Born, caused needless conflict and fuss each morning, hijacking a vaporetto just for the delivery of media summaries to the hotel doors of important people like Frank Carlucci, President Reagan's National Security Advisor. The Dumbest Man Ever Born (DMEB) assured me these summaries were in hot demand at the highest levels, as if DMEB had slept in their rooms with them and observed their morning routines. In reality, the media delivery only disrupted the larger choreography, took one valuable vaporetto out of circulation at a crucial time of day, and was known to anger the White House staff.

The countdown was the enjoyable part. No principals yet, and journalists only beginning to form phalanxes, regiments, armies of inquirers. They didn't need us yet, and we hung out at the beaches and restaurants. We set up little information centers at a Lido hotel, equipped in those early times only with a folding table and chair and a land line. Internet existed only on secret military bases, and clunky cell phones never worked anyway. Someone should have thought of adding pen and paper, but that came only later during the onslaught.

As the Summit got underway the eighth, it was out pretty soon that the 7,000 journalists would be fed decently only with food under a canvas tent, but not with any news they cared about. Stress levels rose as played cards close to their chest. Small press pools posted snarky pool reports for the others on the otherwise bare bulletin boards: "Nancy wearing red today" or "Carpaccio yet again." Frustration and despair set in.

I sat ill-equipped at my station by the folding table, and soon enough the journalists figured out I was part of the problem, not the solution. They gave up begging me for information once they figured out I didn't have any. This didn't please me. We were on eight-hour shifts and took turns being on in the morning, afternoon, and night, for the week we were there.

A day and a half into the Summit, journalists' despair turned to anger. But for the waterways around us they might have stormed the Bastille (the Hotel San Giorgio Maggiore), but you can't exactly storm a hotel from underwater.

My land line rang and I took the call. It was a Soviet broadcaster (the G7 allowed Soviet observers, not participants, that year). Speaking in decent English, he said he'd interviewed every American president since Kennedy, and requested a one-on-one with Secretary of State George Shultz. I took his number and looked for paper to write on, finding only a used envelope someone had left on the folding table.

I passed on the request to State Department spokesman Charles Redman, leaving the scribbled envelope in his hotel room mail slot. Little did I know that SecState Shultz in fact *wanted* to go on Soviet TV that week, less for G7 themes than for the opportunity to address the Soviet people on intermediate-range nuclear weapon (INF) reductions, which were at break point and would soon be finalized. The timing with the G7 was coincidence only.

Redman's answer came back to me that yes, Shultz would grant the interview with a proposed afternoon time the same day. Redman told me the rules for interviews on Soviet TV: no editing; and questions submitted in advance. He said, "Go fix it and show up at the Giorgio Maggiore at 2:00pm."

The journalist chartered a tiny water launch with room just for him, his cameraman, and me. During the 20-minute crossing he said, "How will this work?" I said, "Tell me your questions, I'll write them in English on 3x5 cards for the Secretary to read. While you ask the question in Russian, he'll look at the 3x5 card and then answer in English. Then later you do a voice-over in Russia, for broadcast."

Lacking any better formula, the journalist agreed. When we met Shultz at the Giorgio Maggiore he asked me how the interview would work, and he also agreed to my little plan.

Shultz sought and obtained a Soviet TV audience of 100 million that week in order to convey his message: "This will be the first time in history that two major powers will have voluntarily given up an entire class of weapons." He was very happy, even more so the journalist.

I knew I would have to get out of town quickly not to be lynched by the G7 media who came up with no information at all that week, and who were furious that the only one-on-one from the whole Summit went to Soviet TV, of all places. Word was getting around (falsely of course) that I had sabotaged the free press in G7 countries. My final words at execution would have been, "It wasn't me! It was Chuck Redman!" But that never would have saved me.

When I returned to the hotel at the Lido, I found a torn scrap of paper at my station, the folding table and chair in the lobby. Someone had scribbled "Answer Coming Soon."

I never learned who had left the note, what the question had been, or what the answer might eventually be. The note wasn't signed, and the author never showed up.

This seemed to me the best metaphor for the circumstances, so I kept the paper and later framed it. The little frame sat on my desk for the rest of my 26 years in the Service, following me through six moves until 2009. It was the first item any visitor saw when entering my office. To date it remains the best response I've had for any question, since real questions get no answer on the spot: soon rarely, later if at all, and most of the time never.

Finding Common Ground with Lester
June 2, 2016

We were in the waiting room to meet the governor of Georgia. Amadou K, governor of the Fourth Region of Mali and my charge for his 30-day visit to the U.S., had been high maintenance, and insisted on meeting a U.S. official "of his same rank." The programmer in Washington, exasperated with K's self-inflation, got him a meeting with America's most official racist at the time, Governor Lester Maddox. So there.

Once in the waiting room, I realized this could all unravel quickly. The Washington programmer's joke could backfire, with the ashes and soot landing on me. Maddox, an on-the-record segregationist, was Georgia's 75th governor, the one just before his rival Jimmy Carter, who came in 1970 to take his place. Maddox was wedded to the Confederate flag and openly espoused the agenda of the KKK.

In 1966, Maddox had already made the ax handle an icon with reverberations, famously using one to scare off African-American clients from his Pickrick [sic] fried chicken restaurant. The instrument was popularized and replicated by like-minded activists, as "Pickrick dumstricks." Later he sold miniature souvenir pickaxes as paperweights.

He entertained during his tenure as governor, sometimes riding on a bicycle backwards around the State House.

And there we were, about to spend an hour with him. Good come-uppance for an inflated ego from West Africa, but a pot wanting to boil over from every angle.

The short wait became fifteen minutes. I said to K, "There's something I need to tell you about the governor."

"I know," K said. "A well-known racist. All the more eager to meet him."

I was relieved at least that Governor K knew what he was getting into.

We were ushered in, and the governors were friendly off the bat. Each sought, with success, to charm the other. At the time I wondered why and how, but my job was to interpret words (French), not meanings.

They were jovial from both sides and lacked only a theme to follow. I guess for Maddox, K was a "just-passing-through," and got his respect and attention. The lacking theme took only a few minutes to come out: both men had passionate interest in piloting small airplanes – Maddox for recreation, K for needs of the job, since his province was the size of Virginia and had no real roads.

Lester was enchanted to become K's mentor on the purchase and piloting of small aircraft in the United States. There were Cessnas, Lairds, Beechcrafts, Curtis-Wrights, Lakes, and others.

Maddox owned one, and knew most of the others. The following week, K and I would be at the Cessna plat in Wichita. He fell in love with the three-seater whose salesman took us up for a test drive through the clouds, including a heart-in-throat stall (*"Maintenant on va caller l'avion,"* I said, before thinking to myself "I'm not paid enough to do this").

Back to Atlanta. Maddox coached Governor K on aircraft and I think was the one to win him over to Cessnas. The hour ended most cordially, and at the end Governor Maddox walked us to his door. As an afterthought he handed one of his signature ax-head paperweights to K as a memento. He smiled for a split second, thinking he might have committed a gaffe, or maybe meant to.

"I thank you, Governor," K said. "And I will treasure this gift."

The minds had met, and for a single hour, the two individuals focused on what they had in common, forgetting or disregarding who and what they were.

While I Was Out of Town
June 6, 2016

Here is what's left of the Dynasty Hotel in Malabo, Equatorial Guinea. It was the second best in the city in 2006, when I stayed there. Of the best one, the Bahia, not even rubble remains.

Now for comparison, here is the Sofitel, the second best hotel today, 2016:

No value judgments here, but I don't know another city which could have changed so much in ten years. Maybe not even in China. Now, in 2016, woods and grass plots have turned to new ministry buildings, the Spanish colonial remains of the former Santa Isabel have been cleaned and trimmed. New state-of-the-art hotels have popped up, and a whole city of villas remains waiting at the outskirts for heads of state to stay during future summits.

The "ministries" section of the city, meant to dazzle, is mostly two to three years old, some much less. I've heard the narrative about building used for the purpose of money laundering, the Chinese getting a foothold for ulterior motives, and the rest. But the physical progress is not a mirage. You can't ignore it.

Equatorial Guinea ("EG") has the advantage of having a small population, some 1.3 million. It has a crazy geography, with the capital on the island of Bioko (formerly Fernando Po) and a good chunk of its people and commerce on the mainland a couple of hundred miles away. I remember standing on the back patio of the Bahia in 2006, looking at Cameroon across the water, not far away. I thought, "Why is this even a country?" And yes, it has the dumb luck of having oil and natural gas, with the advantages of huge revenues years ago (never distributed to the people, to be fair). But the decline in oil and gas market prices has left the country vulnerable, and yet the buildings and private company headquarters continue to pour in. Venezuela has been unable to deal with these fluctuations, and even Saudi Arabia and Russia have had their tumults, where EG is making its way.

The U.S. government does not like the human rights situation in EG, and has said so publicly in its Human Rights Report for 2015. The HRR recounts some grisly behavior, though probably forty countries come in worse.

I have no reason to airbrush this quirky little country, but I note its physical beauty. Surely people live way below the poverty line in the midst of the opulence of some, but in crisscrossing Bioko island I saw nothing as shocking as downtown Baltimore. Even the villages have reliable electricity; I saw it myself.

There's a lot of talk and action in EG about saving the environment, yet primeval forests undulate through the countryside with immense trees that no one is yet felling for profit. These are not baobobs, but "ceiba," some of which climb 200 feet high and don't seem bothered by the vines growing up their trunks.

In the Dutch-curse stampede years ago to get the oil and gas out, cacao production was more or less abandoned. But lucky them, it could be brought back at any time. There is no lack of land, and property rights are pretty well documented. Poor people can own and cultivate it. The rainy seasons irrigate verdant fields and forests, where nearly anything grows.

Small as the country is, there remain two worlds within: the privileged and well connected, and the others. Discontent no doubt is near and beneath the surface, but desperation, demeaning poverty, and disease do not appear in the streets or, for that matter, in the villages on the Island. Six-lane highways accommodate a trickle of vehicle traffic, waiting I suppose for periods of more general well-being. The latter may come, maybe not. But planning has made it possible.

Drexel University is here, from Philadelphia, running graduate programs on environment, and the Wildlife Conservation Society is saving tortoises from extinction.

The current government in Malabo is friendly with North Korea and with Jean-Marie Le Pen. I don't know the logic in this, but there may be one. The Chinese architecture mushrooming in the city is not vulgar or immense, but fits into an aesthetic consistency of its own. No perfect right angles, fortunately. Every complex has its own little motif. The Chinese are no doubt getting lots in return, but maybe they deserve it.

I'm neither ignoring nor focusing on the hidden agendas beneath the surface here, and the inequities. But "the worst place in the world" is rivaled by other, more suited ones. There is cognitive dissonance. If you come expecting horror, you'll have to adjust expectations.

I don't claim I can make sense of all this. I know only that there was a place called "Malabo" which I saw in 2006, and another by the same name now. Nothing much in common, and make of that what you will.

Trash Tree in Malabo

June 9, 2016

All humans' stories are engaging, some are astounding. Here is Plácido Guimaraes, aka "Pocho," community artist in Equatorial Guinea's capital, Malabo.

Pocho left his country during the extrajudicial killings of the 1970s and made his way to Spain, the former colonizing country of his own. After five years there, he moved to Ukraine, where he studied urban architecture. In the 1980s he went back to Spain, this time to Valencia, where he looked at how to work textiles into theater, dance, and film. When the coast cleared a bit in the 1990s, he returned to Equatorial Guinea to "rediscover his roots."

He is a man of language and spatial twists. Earth Day 2016 was themed "Trees for the Planet," and a community park called Alcaide was spruced up (pun forgiven, I hope) for the occasion. Embassies, oil companies, community activists joined to clear and paint the area on a Saturday morning, working around a live soccer game on the field. Trees went up, garbage was removed. It was a tiny gesture in a yearly tradition started in 1970. The political climate in the United States was different back then. A Democrat from Wisconsin (Gaylord Nelson) and a Republican Congressman (Pete McCloskey) cosponsored the first celebration. Bipartisan, imagine! Now 100 countries participate, and (supposedly) over a billion individuals in their various places. If this is more or less true, it would be the largest community (virtual) gathering in history.

Working quickly to execute a concept he had in advance, the artist had the idea to celebrate garbage's removal by immortalizing the garbage itself as a tree. A good joke on degradation, to exalt it. The tree here pictured has no natural materials, but is made of metal, cables, wire, and fragments of discarded plastic water bottles.

And here it remains – after a week, anyway. Solid, adapted to change, likely to endure. Ominous clouds in the background contrast the burst of sunlight on the "tree" itself. Not to hyperventilate here, but note the same principles at work in Rembrandt's "Windmill," now on view at the National Gallery in Washington, DC.

Real trees are not symbols, but are loved for themselves. This lovely, phony one, entirely symbolic, will show up little in nature but lots in people's imaginations and memories.

I don't know if trees in clusters sense community, but humans have communities solely by sensing them. On some occasions a lifted spirit turns the community's attention to itself, through depiction, humor, and the physical markers that guide people's attention and memories. It has to do with survival, since the alternatives are stark.

Walking Dschang
June 13, 2016

I don't remember his name, but here he was in 1979. I trust he's well and prospering now.

"Dschang" sounds like a province in China, but it's a hilly retreat in northwestern Cameroon, where the French *colons* used to go to cool off. Dschang is the last French-speaking town before you get to the English-speaking provinces to the west and north. I'm told it is an overpopulated metropolis now, but in 1979 it was a Shangri-la of savanna, favored by sun, water, and breezes. There were cottages for rent, the Centre Climatique de Dschang, run by a genial French couple.

I had one hour of work in Dschang, then parked myself for three days until the next plane out.

There were nature trails. They weren't labeled so. The walking was good, so I did a lot of it. On my second hike up the hill from the Centre Climatique, I noticed a young boy following me, so I thought my privacy might be breached. I don't mind being followed as long as the ulterior motives are clear. I put some small bills in my shirt pocket, and considered giving the boy some money and asking him if I might continue on my own.

He was mainly just curious, and hadn't seen many out-of-towners. He studied me as I guess an anthropologist would, putting algorithmic matrices over my patterns.

I was the first to break the silence. He did have questions, but no requests. He wanted to know how and why a stranger lands in Dschang, and what in the world can be found outside of that town.

I said I was from Washington in the United States. About twice a day I walked, and he always appeared. As he had legitimate questions, I thought I might answer some of the easier ones. Back in my room I found a post card of Washington, and took it with me on the second day to show him. The child was puzzled at the photo, which showed an equestrian statue on the west slope below the U.S. Congress.

"*C'est quoi?*" he asked.

"*C'est une statue,*" I answered. He looked more puzzled.

"*Statue?*" The concept was not familiar.

"It's like a man and a horse, but not really," I explained. "More an imitation. Made of metal, marble, that sort of thing."

Photos were familiar to him, large buildings and statues not. He had heard of horses but had never seen one.

We went a further distance up the path, and at this point we walked together. I preferred this to being shadowed and spooked from behind.

I realized his world was about as unfamiliar to me as mine was to him. "Is that a coffee plant?" I said, pointing to a green patch near the walking trail.

He found this genuinely funny, that a person from the greater world could know so little about his.

"That's avocado!" he said, laughing. I laughed also.

I almost redeemed myself by spotting a eucalyptus tree on the horizon. I recognized it from trips to California. He beamed with a teacher's pride, noting my potential, and ability to name at least one significant plant.

"You have those in your country?" he smiled.

"We do," I answered. "But you don't see them every day." I meant, in California yes, in Washington probably not.

The boy processed this information and looked a bit troubled. My answer was not logical, and lacked information. After a few minutes running the facts through his filter, he said, "You say you have them in your country but don't see them every day?"

"That's right," I said.

He put two and two together: "So in your country, the trees.... *walk*?"

I laughed because his logic was watertight; he had nailed me. I explained that "don't see every day" can mean that the observer changed positions, not the trees, just like in Dschang. He seemed relieved to be freed from arcane new patterns, and joined me in laughter.

We became friends. He taught me about his lovely environment. In a child's natural way, he had pride in being able to teach something to an older person.

The three days were up and I went on my way to the next stops on my itinerary, and then home to Washington.

Weeks later the boy and my time with him haunted me. I wrote to the French couple who ran the Centre Climatique, and slipped in a copy of the photo in the envelope. I asked if they might help me locate the boy and give him bits of money for school. I should have figured out earlier more about him and where to find him.

The French couple sent me a polite letter back. Notwithstanding my good motives, they said, the mission made no sense: any money coming the way of the boy's house would be taken by the father and never get to where we all wanted it to be.

I got the point, and dropped the effort. No need to stir the pot in a community with its own ways.

The boy and my brief time with him still haunt me, and suggest that even good connections with people have a limited shelf life.

I wish the boy well, now that he would be 35 or 40 years old. I hope he never got AIDS and has had a chance to used his crafty logic and thirst for information. Of all human tools, these matter the most.

Restless
June 21, 2016

Here is the ugliest building in Spain, aka the American Embassy in Madrid.

Spain's architecture was sort of rudimentary until the Roman period. The latter produced Romanesque churches, many of which you can see today. The conquering Visigoths were not scorched earth types, and appreciated these exquisite structures, adding their own style as an overlay.

The Muslim conquest in 711 improved on the Romanesque and Visigoth eras, adding their own Umayyad marvels. The Umayyads ran into hard times in the 1080s, and called in the Almoravids in 1086 to help them hold the line against advancing Christians. The Almoravids obliged but in fact took over 1162-1269. Even as they did so, they ran into competing Almohads, a sort of Muslim Puritan or Reformationist twelfth-century movement favoring simplicity in building styles. Though austere, the latter introduced brick as a medium of construction, and completed the masterwork of the Great Mosque of Córdoba in 1148 (begun by Umayyads in 785).

The Almohads made Seville their capital, a city which later became Europe's largest. Before they were quite finished, the Almoravids sent troops north to take Europe, but were stopped by The Cid in 1100 (or Roland, depending on which version you follow). The Almoravids (think "Roccoco") continued to add yet more graceful layers to the mix, such as the Giralda (originally a minaret) of Seville, and later the Alhambra of Grenada in 1237. Meanwhile the Christians took Córdoba in 1236 and built a church *over* the Great Mosque. Every time something happened, the buildings became more graceful and decorative.

The Almoravids, notwithstanding Almohad competition in areas of the Peninsula, retained the separate Kingdom of Granada, superseded but not removed by the Christian Reconquista of 1492.

Unconverted Muslims ("morsiscos") permitted to stay in the Kingdom until 1609 enhanced the aesthetic blend yet further in the Mudéjar style, which only improved the architectural output through fusion and diversity. Taken together, the Umayyads, and Almoravids, Almohads, and Mudéjars are sometimes just called "The Moors." These were no slouches, and introduced stringed instruments to Europe. You could trace a squiggly line between the earliest lutes and rebecs to the Mannheim school of orchestral interpretation.

Political and military convulsions resulted in the embellishment, not destruction or iconoclasm, of earlier masterpieces. The uneasy but fruitful coexistence drew on Iberia's three cultures – Christian, Muslim, and Jewish. Santa Maria la Blanca in Toledo, originally a synagogue built by Muslims, later became a church, theologically but not aesthetically disruptive.

Building and architecture remained Spain's glory and genius, yielding from the Roman, Visigoth, Almoravid, Mudéjar, and other blends to the Christian Renaissance, Baroque, Spanish colonial, and neo-classical periods, each adding to the foundations of earlier masters and revering their predecessors even as they sought to better them.

Post-Reconquest churches in Córdoba and Granada made a point of meticulous preservation of the mosques that preceded them, and adding the Catholic paraphernalia physically *on top* of the earlier Muslim style so as to underscore their primacy. This building on top of preceding works demonstrated obeisance to predecessors, with improvement, not removal, their goal.

Spain never stopped producing. Later came Catalan *modernismo* and Gaudí, and more recently, many dozens of world leaders, including visionaries such as Enrique Nieto, Alonzo Cano, Jaume Busquets, Josep Lluis Sert, Antonio Palacios, the current Santiago Calatrava, and others.

Which brings us full circle to the U.S Embassy in Madrid, an unprovoked insult and indignity in an otherwise lovely cityscape. Circa 1960, this wretched eyesore was put up without permanence in mind, and in the spirit of planned obsolescence. Then it refused to be obsolete, though it should have been.

The condo-beige concrete slabs forming the façade began to disintegrate in 2015. Instead of razing the thing and considering a fresh start, the Overseas Building Office (OBO) of the Department of State decided to repair and replace the failing surface, now (June 2016) into its fourteenth month of *obras*.

Spanish employees in the building wear protective helmets (yes, helmets) to shield themselves from falling debris, and strap on face masks to protect against black lung disease, with dust now everywhere in the interior. They have been putting up with this for over a year.

America does have a culture and even great numbers of graceful architectural achievements in its homeland. It saves its horrors for export, like tobacco and DDT. We shouldn't do this to friends.

Madrid puts together immodesty and grace, as few other capitals do. Everywhere are reminders that this was once an empire that vied with all others. These blend with the charm of a thousand little eateries and places to while away a spring or summer afternoon, some of them still sparkling with decorative tiles from the nineteenth century.

Ingrained in the Spanish character is a certain indifference to the past, but a pattern going back 1,500 years, of letting it be and encouraging it to speak for itself.

Despite current economic hardship, Madrid is one of the safest capitals in Europe. You can meander down a dark alley in most neighborhoods in the early morning hours without needing to look over your shoulder. People will assist the lost tourist and seek to please the diner from abroad. Anyone will wish you *buen día* ("Have a good day") when the elevator stops at their floor before yours.

Madrileños live and let live, but are not bland. They stress and smoke and seem dissatisfied. This quality takes them a step above serenity, to disquiet, and adds pizzazz to a city which must sleep at some point, but it hasn't come clear when they do so. You can see this in the wandering eyes and spirited hangovers of the characters in Pedro Almodóvar's films.

Of the many misfortunes to befall us if/when the sun collides with the earth, not the least would be the destruction of the city of Madrid.

My point is not so much our aggressive assaults on Spain's lovely culture, but Spaniards' seemingly limitless willingness to forgive, to charm and let bygones go. It may not last forever; at some point patience could run out. I don't know how we keep managing to borrow more time on people's good nature, apparently unaware that the unpaid bills of aesthetic offense may one day come due.

Ambassador to the Mountain
June 28, 2016

Each one of them thought he was better than his predecessor. In a way each one was, but none of them ever really got the hang of it.

This one had been to fancy schools and strategy courses, and took himself to be a smarty-pants. Everyone gets a fresh start and the benefit of the doubt at the beginning, at least. That's the meaning of the System.

This one came with pre-cooked ideas of how to solve intractable problems that had stumped the ones before him. He called me into his office one mid-morning. The Department issued fresh statements daily, devoid of impact or meaning, mistaking themselves to be solemn pronouncements of the great Ralph Bunche, now long gone.

"How does this look to you?" he said, handing me a page of text.

I read the half page meant for public distribution. I handed it back to him and said, "The usual flatulence, sir."

"Well I wrote it," he answered. He liked candor and never held my comment against me. Au contraire.

After four months of slamming into walls, he demonstrated to himself and others that his mental constructs made no more sense than any of his predecessors'.

He said at Country Team, exasperated, "Okay, so now what do we do?"

He had the intellectual rigor to know he had reached a dead end. The situation demanded something entirely new.

"It's probably time to meet Jake," I said, referring to the eccentric American writer up in the hills above the city. Jake had seen the diplomats and development experts come and go, come and go, each one of them erased from memory from the day they left. He was a stringer for a wire service, and had lived on the mountain for 18 years, seeing all.

The ambassador's shoulders slumped, because he knew I was right, and this came with a sting of humiliation. "You're right. Bring him over to the house Wednesday." He looked away, dreading a little what was in store.

"Sorry, sir, but he's been to that house too many times before. You'll have to go and see him at his."

The ambassador slumped yet lower. He knew there was no way around it.

Jake gave each newcomer a chance not to be stupid, because he did want better things for this wrecked country. He loved the place and tried to combat his own pessimism, but it was getting harder each year to do so. The Americans were present in the minds of all the locals, but the Americans thought in parallelograms and parabolas that never matched local thinking. They always hit dead ends, and Jake probably knew better. Anyway, he was glad to be asked.

The day I went to pick up the ambassador at his residence, I saw he was smarter than most: he understood he'd have to wear jeans and a T-shirt if he were to get anything out of the meeting on the mountain. I was impressed that he caught onto this without needing to be told.

We got in back of his armored SUV and headed up the mountain at sunset. He would have asked me how to make the most of this, but he already got it: listen, don't talk. Just this once.

When we got to the alleyway that led to Jake's sort-of house (more a shack), we found the SUV was too wide to slip between the rocks and building remains by the road. So we got out and walked the last 100 feet, now in darkness. There was almost never electricity in the neighborhood, and the ambassador caught on quickly to the importance of seeing how normal people lived, the majority without the generators he had. He was not (yet) daunted.

Jake met us at the door eagerly, and walked us to the back balcony, which jutted out over a populated gorge below. You could sense and even hear the multitudes, but couldn't see anything in the darkness.

There was a single light bulb on the balcony, lit by a system of car batteries Jake had jerry-rigged, so as to keep a single light bulb going, and enough current to send his wire story drafts over the Internet. He slept under a ceiling fan. When the city electricity went on at unpredictable times in the night (a couple of times a week), the fan would wake him up and he'd go over to plug the car batteries to the wall outlet and charge them. That way he always had enough power for the light bulb and the Internet connection to headquarters in New York. He hadn't been to his native United States in over fifteen years, so this was normal for him.

We settled on the back balcony, where bugs swarmed around the single light bulb.

The ambassador wanted—needed—solutions and answers. He understood he would have to humble himself to get them. He became upset when Jake didn't supply any at all, not even suggestions.

"Sir, you're welcome to try like the others, but as I see it, you'll be lucky if you can get your people out of here alive. That's the best you can hope for."

The ambassador was quick to exasperation, not to anger. "That can't be the best there is," he said.

"Maybe you can do better," Jake said, putting tobacco into his pipe. "But none of the others ever did, and I don't think you will either."

The chat went on for about 90 minutes. Jake had the upper part of the dialogue almost all the time, with the ambassador only asking the occasional question. I respected him for those rare moments of humility.

At one point Jake said, "There are two books you'll want to read, in order to understand this place."

The ambassador pulled out a pen and paper. It was too dark to see, but he knew he could write a few words and make sense of it later. He looked to Jake for what came next.

"*Exodus*," Jake said. The ambassador wrote it down.

"You mean the novel? Leon Uris?"

"No. You know, the second book of the Old Testament. It's about how a national identity is forged only once a traumatized generation dies off after 40 years in the desert. The people here never had that luxury."

"Okay." the ambassador said. "And the second book?"

"*Alice in Wonderland*. The only way I know of, to understand how the logic works here." He lit his pipe.

The ambassador never wrote that one down, and didn't like being taken for a fool. Quietly he folded the paper and stuffed it back in his pocket.

The conversation ran its course; the evening was over. The ambassador got up, thanked Jake for the warm ginger ale, and took me back with him to the SUV waiting out in the street.

He was rattled, and needed decompression. He took me to a neighborhood bar where he could process what he had heard. "Not acceptable," he said. He didn't blame me.

"But anyway we heard him out. It was the right thing to do."

At this point another American expat walked up to the ambassador. Most of us knew Alec the Beltway Bandit working on AID contracts. But the ambassador hadn't been in country long enough to meet him.

Alec, more than half soused, walked up to the ambassador hiding behind his jeans and T-shirt.

"Ha, so you're the new ambassador here," he said, laughing. "And you probably think you can do any better than the others." With a bony finger he poked the ambassador in the shoulder, and walked away, laughing even harder.

Nowhere to hide. The ambassador got home and regained his composure, and, after a few days, even his self-confidence. But he never managed to do anything of worth in the three years that followed. Americans were not killed under his watch, but later a few were.

Managing Information Technology for a New Us

July 11, 2016

Times are difficult, and polarized silos exist. It is more important than ever for differing cultures to understand and accept one another.

For IT providers and IT consumers, wide gulfs of misunderstanding create false impressions of antagonism. These stumbling blocks are easily remedied with sensitive, mutual understanding and some basics in vocabulary building.

Follows, a primer in what to say and think in order to enhance collaborative confidence building.

For the IT consumer:

1. They explain what they do, but not in a language you understand.

2. They relate to other people in ways not familiar to you.

3. They think we see them as unable to explain what they do or relate to other people.

4. Do not offend them by showing what you think of them; they already know what you think.

5. For them, thinking what you think of them is a self-fulfilling prophesy.

6. Do not flatter them too much, since they will think you are trying to beguile or get special favors.

7. Do not insult them by saying directly what you need.

8. You need not try not to offend them, since they already believe that you think badly of them.

9. Do not think of them as "the others," since this will create misunderstanding.

10. Somehow let them know you appreciate what they do, since no one else ever does.

11. Do not actually say you appreciate them, since they will see this with suspicion as an effort to undermine their expertise.

12. Understand that their area of authority is circumscribed and may not apply to other aspects of life.

13. Never let them think that you see their area of expertise as circumscribed, since they will be offended.

14. Do not try to understand them, since they will take that an act of aggression.

15. It's complicated.

For the IT provider:

1. Be patient with the uneven backgrounds of your clients. Some have no aptitude for the tools

they so fundamentally need. These will quickly make themselves known.

2. The ones who intensify their pleas show themselves thereby to be unteachable. If you are a Calvinist, turn your attention to someone more worthy.

3. Know that they see your knowledge as an assertion of power over them. They are very insecure individuals.

4. Never answer a question the first time.

5. Never answer a question that was not asked with the correct vocabulary. Pretending not to understand will advance the learning process.

6. Beware of clients seeming to be cordial toward you; they do so only from desperation.

7. Do not be misled by flattery; it comes with hidden agendas.

8. Hidden agendas become clear when the clients are under stress.

9. Do not accept rudeness as a consequence of urgency.

10. *Dignitatis super omnium et inter alia.*

11. Remind the clients of their dependencies. With humility (for them) will come wisdom.

12. Do not seek to humiliate them, for they will resent you.

13. Do not stand in their way when they humiliate themselves. Karma will lead them to where they should be.

14. To their stress, respond only with serenity.

15. If they are ungrateful and arrogant, their path to self-fragmentation is established without extra efforts on your part.

16. Do not mistake their gestures of kindness as anything other than desperation.

17. Know they are saying things behind your back. Do not descend to their level.

18. At all times demonstrate your devotion to service. Seek nothing in return.

19. If an IT program should not work, blame it on the hardware.

Uh Oh, Nativism is Not Only Offensive

July 18, 2016

There are plenty of smart people in Washington, none smarter than International Monetary Fund Managing Director Christine Lagarde. Also, her friend Nancy Birdsall, who created the Center for Global Development fifteen years ago. CGD is one of the few think-tanks in Washington that believes in something ("development is possible"). Most of the others will tell you what cannot be done.

These two thinkers demonstrated this July 14 at CGD, a couple of hours before the attacks in Nice. As many times before, they showed that brains will help if we are to resolve the inequities that frustrate both us and the crazies. Shedding brains for ego, rhetoric, impulse, appetite, fly catching, tribalism will likely not. We are in real trouble here. This common perception may unite us at some point.

Challenges, Lagarde said, are low growth, rising inequality, and falling numbers of jobs. Resolve these three stumbling blocks and we may get the world to work better. The IMF alone cannot do it, nor even the IMF, World Bank, U.S. government, OECD, European Union, and United Nations together. We can't channel the human mind to a higher level anytime soon, but we'd better tackle those three bugbears or we're all sunk. The wealthy with the others.

Lagarde reminded us that the sixty low income countries make up one-fifth of the world's population. You don't have to like them if you don't care to. These are the ones who will vote with their feet and land on our doorsteps. Interdiction cannot prevent them when they lack options to stay at home. The UN's Sustainable Development Goals (SDGs) established in 2015 are well and good, but only if implemented.

The good news, she said, is that 1.4 billion people rose out of "abject" poverty from 2000 to 2015, child mortality fell, and there was progress in eradication of malaria, HIV/AIDS, and tuberculosis. The least developed countries advanced by six per cent in growth. Nice. "I was prepared to wear my happy-face," Lagarde said, before getting to the bad news:

Fragile states grew only at 2-3 per cent, and of the 60 least developed countries, only sixteen met their targets of poverty reduction. Demographic increases, climate change, and violent conflict (civil war and terrorism) stand in the way – not surprisingly, and evidence increases that humans have taken what the Enlightenment called "happiness" and managed to throw it do the dogs.

Something called "sound macroeconomic management" aims for low inflation, low debt, fiscal probity, competitive exchange rates, and reduction of public debt. Fair enough. Official development assistance (ODA) must rise from the 0.3 per cent it is now to 0.7 per cent. This is not altruism, but the sort of planning that can address desperate migration, pandemics, public coffers disappearing into offshore account,s and tax evasion, leaving the rest of us to our potholes, rising crime rates, kidnappings which will only increase and spoil our European vacations. And yes, terrorism. This is caca we do not need or want, and it is getting ever closer to our protected enclosures. No one escapes. We needn't be generous souls to see that our fouled nest should be at least deodorized.

Since 1996 the IMF has provided $76 billion in debt relief to Heavily

Indebted, Poor Countries (HIPC), but this is a water spider on the surface of a pond of algae scum.

Most poignantly, nativism will not take anyone forward, not even the nativists. "Do not revert within borders," Lagarde said July 14, choosing her words carefully and avoiding political gaffes like the recent one of Justice Ruth Bader Ginsburg. Christine Lagarde never commits gaffes. Listen to her and heed her, or else.

Otherwise, prepare to raise the ramparts and spike the multitudes with baseball bats and fly-swatters. They, too, can get nasty. We see how adept they are at learning to do so. We are nowhere much in solving or even addressing the challenges we face. Urgency and prudence. Demagogues can be ignored or countered, but distractions from the closing circle of deadlines for getting it right will not wait while we peruse, vent, and get angry at certain despicable individuals seeking to lead us.

Arounothay's Tux
July 25, 2016

Arounothay was a survivor of the Laotian holocaust of the 1970s. An economist, he was my upstairs neighbor at the university apartments in Brazzaville, the capital of the Little Congo. It's hard to imagine a more misplaced individual, but he was teaching economics in a Marxist country (Marxist in name only). Of the horrors of the twentieth century, the Pathet Lao in Vientiane were up at the top in cruelty and murderous social engineering.

There were three units in the little chalet those days in 1980. I lived on the ground floor, Arounothay on the floor above. Modest but tidy. Running water was mainly stuck in the city's antiquated pipe system; if you left a bucket in the early morning under a neighborhood tap, the bucket would be about half-full by late afternoon. Expats respected one another's buckets; in fact I don't remember one ever being removed while we were out at the university campus a few miles away. You learned to make do with a half bucket a day for washing dishes, showering, and boiling corn and rice. It wasn't all that bad.

Once, everyone in the neighborhood went down to the water works on mopeds to try to intimidate the authorities into fixing the pipes. But we didn't really look like a motorcycle gang, and the managers mainly ignored us. The next day, a leafy branch was planted in the roadway leading to the chalets – meaning "men at work." But they went no farther toward getting water flowing in the neighborhood. The little branch was kind of a thumbed nose.

Parking a moped inside the house was against the rules, but it would have been folly to have the 'ped and gas tank out on the entrance to the building. In fact, the one time I forgot to bring it in behind the double-locked gate, sure enough it was gone the next morning. I went to the police station just to report the theft. When I entered, a prisoner was walking behind the counter with one of the police; the commander said, "Put this man in jail for stealing a Mobylette."

I said, "What did he have to do with it?"

"Maybe nothing," said the police chief. "But either way, he's guilty of something."

And oh yes, Arounothay. He was always cheerful, usually laughing about one thing or another.

He walked around in a small bathing suit, which he called "my tux."

He had been director of the electricity company in Laos before the Pathet Lao took over in 1975. He'd been sent to one of the internment camps that few survived. His wife was taken to another. After a year or so of enslavement and daily beatings, he withered to a skeletal frame. Even when I knew him five years later, he was so small he seemed like about half a person.

They had labored in the fields and then were taken to shout Marxist slogans in the late afternoon before getting their daily, tiny bowl of rice. Many starved; others were killed with garden instruments and firearms. No one expected to make it out alive.

One day they found Arounothay in the fields, and managed to

identify him. The Pathet Lao had realized they didn't know how to run an electrical plant, and retrieved him from the camp to get him back to his former work.

They spent a few months taking him around in a limousine and feeding him to fatten him up. It was no honor to be picked out of a death camp, and was also ominous since the regime was capricious. They told him to just sleep and eat and mind his business.

Even during those confused days he wore his bathing suit, which he called "my tux." His minders in the regime drove him through the city but never told him if his wife was alive or dead. It would have been stupid to ask.

After a few months they put him back to work at the electricity plant. No illusions here: perform or die. Arounothay used to laugh as he told me his story. It was partly the Third World laughter everywhere in the world, directed at irremediable hardship. It was also from his good nature.

One day his wife was delivered back to him without explanation. She'd been in a separate camp, and had also defied the odds and survived. They walked together one day near a bridge over the Mekong River.

A friendly Canadian diplomat came up to them and said in a very soft voice, "Go now, cross the bridge, and we will pick you up on the other side. Just go now."

So it was that Arounothay and his wife made it out of their homeland hell, to Vietnam, and somehow from there on to France.

In the 1960s Arounothay had done an advanced degree in economics, so the French government picked him to do a *"coopération,"* teaching in Africa so as to keep a hand in the former colonies.

He had learned conventional econ – macro, micro, market forces, things like that. This did not jive with the national university of a Marxist country. He taught what he knew. I thought for sure he would be expelled from the country. I kept a low profile myself, teaching English language.

"I'll be fine," he used to say, always laughing.

"But the bureaucrats here don't like what you're teaching," I said.

"And what if they don't?"

I knew that death camps were worse than expulsion, but still I thought he was being a little foolhardy, and told him so. *"Ne t'en fais pas,"* he would always answer. Don't worry about it.

His stories evolved until he came back to the house, saying that a few of the advanced students had told him they liked what he was teaching, and could he please tell them more.

Gradually his Western concepts took root until the junior Congolese faculty members showed an interest as well. Eventually, market economics came to prevail in the department. This was concerning to the political officers running the university. Oh shit, I thought.

He was convoked to a sort of inquisition, and ordered to explain himself.

"I know Marxist economy. If it's the Marxist catechism you want, I know I can do it better than you, since I did it on my knees for hours every afternoon in the camp in Laos. But if you want real economics, keep me here and I will provide it. Your choice."

Exasperated, the authorities let him be, and he made it through a three-year stint as a French employee in the Université Marien Ngouabi. He built a following for himself.

Then he packed up and moved back to a suburb north of Paris. I visited him here a few years later. "You have done marvelously," I said.

"I still have my tux," he said. "The one I wore in the camp, and around the house in Brazzaville." It was cold in Paris that day, but Arounothay's smile was the same as it had been, four degrees below the Equator.

Why I Learned French

August 8, 2016

Nineteen sixty-six, and I was flunking French. I don't mean "doing badly," but as in, getting straight Fs. The first assignment that freshman year was to read 70 pages of *Le Rouge et le Noir* of Stendhal, and to do it within 48 hours. They might as well have put me in an advanced Indonesian, for the preparation I had.

I went to my advisor and said I was in the wrong course. He looked it up and said, "No you're not. The placement exam has you at this level." To this day I'm convinced I had skipped a question on the multiple-choice test and inadvertently got a series of answers right, when they shouldn't have been.

"No I mean seriously," I said.

"Sorry. You'll have to stay where you are."

My head spun. I'd done pretty well in high school in general, but never gave much attention to French and never learned much of it. College was serious business back then. No buffets or rock climbing on expensive jungle gyms.

It was confounding. The war in Vietnam was not going well, and college dropouts were highly in demand to fill the ranks. This was not a conflict I was committed to.

The scenario was as follows: flunk one course at the end of the semester and go on probation, do it again, then be asked to leave. Pass a physical exam, enter the infantry, travel to Vietnam and murder a few children, then come back a paraplegic if at all. This was not the guaranteed sequence, but it was possible.

I was cornered. I had come to college to learn English literature and psychology, like all the pre-Birkenstocks. Not much originality in that.

So the choice was clear enough: learn French very quickly or get ready for boot camp.

Many people in history have learned French under duress, but I don't know if anyone had more motivation than I did. I quadrupled my time looking up words and trying to figure out verb tenses and prepositions. It took a lot of effort in a short time, and I ended up having none at all left over for English or psych, which I never enrolled in after all.

My F went to D-minus, then D, and so forth until it seemed I had the hang of it. No motivation like survival.

Learning that quickly did get me going, though, so I thought, What the hell, I might as well major in it. Then other French-related things happened later.

I just wanted to clear the record on this, because people sometimes ask. I hear young people these days talking about their "passion," which I thought was what Jesus did when he became Christ. I think people talking about passions these days are mainly faking it.

I don't exactly espouse fear as motivator, but real or imagined, it does create an industrious approach to surmounting tasks.

The fears of those times at least were founded and not random as they are these days. Conflicts since the invention of gunpowder have involved a lot of shooting into bushes, for terror of what may be invisible and lurking within. Most of these bullets have missed their mark, since there really were no marks to start with.

My point is more the nature of anxiety, rather than the folly of war. I wish courage and success to those who must now vanquish enemies—including unknown, bizarre market forces—which they have never had the advantage of seeing. The nimble will inherit the Earth, even if it's an inheritance they never asked for.

Kindly Make Sense of This

August 12, 2016

We pack suitcases and luggage racks, getting ready for fall on America's campuses. Time to reflect and take stock. Somebody's doing some self-wounding here. Friends help friends with interventions, before addiction wins out.

Maybe you've heard that there is student debt in the United States. Intellectuals say there may be a political solution to this. Yes, and Saturn's moon Titan may have life that breathes nitrogen instead of oxygen. It's possible.

Debt is the symptom of a calamity; cost is the cause. The twirly-moustache types setting the prices don't even bother hiding behind grass stalks. Why should they, if no one is looking? One day, someone will ask, "What were you doing during the academic wars?" Somebody help me understand, meanwhile, why college students and their parents are not out there with pitchforks.

Just some basic stats, in case you didn't know about this:

Over half (some say 75 per cent) of college courses are taught by adjuncts. (Nothing against adjuncts! Bear with me while we get through the stats.)

Adjuncts earn $2-3,000 per semester course. (Nothing unfair about this! If someone wants to sell a new Tesla for 2.5 bananas, no one should stand in the way.)

College tuition has increased by four percent compounded, since 1995.

> The average tuition and fees at private national universities rose during that period by 179 percent.
> Out-of-state tuition and fees at public universities rose 226 percent.
> In-state tuition and fees at public national universities increased 296 percent.
> [source: U.S. News and World Report. See other sources for comparables, if you want.]

The U.S. government Bureau of Labor Statistics (BLS) reports that for 2015, college and university administrators earned a median pay of $88,580 per year, while instructors earned twenty percent less. By the way, instructors are outnumbered by administrators three to two. Administrative positions on campus grew 60 per cent 1993 to 2009, ten times more than tenured faculty positions. [source: U.S. Department of Education]

What do administrators do on college campuses? Don't take my word for it, read the profile by the BLS:

> Decide if potential students should be admitted to the school;
> Schedule and register students for classes;
> Schedule space and times for classes;
> Ensure that students meet graduation requirements;
> Plan commencement ceremonies;
> Prepare transcripts and diplomas for students;
> Produce data about students and classes;
> Maintain the academic records of the institution;
> Advise students on topics such as housing issues, personal problems, or academics;

> Communicate with parents or guardians;
> Create, support, and assess nonacademic programs for students;
> Schedule programs and services, such as athletic events or recreational activities.

Catch-and-release programs recruit a maximum number of applicants, so as to increase the number of rejected freshmen. (Recruiters are well paid to jack up these numbers.) This raises the college rankings in the U.S. News and World Report.

Instructors, by contrast, instruct.

Crunch, then, some numbers creatively but accurately. In a private university, students pay up to $2,000 per credit hour, or $6,000 per typical three-hour course. So, at 25 students per class section, the university takes in, say, $150,000 per section. The instructor, usually an adjunct, gets $2-3,000 of the $150,000, or can otherwise volunteer the time instead, to maintain some dignity.

You may spend four years and earn a bachelor's degree. If you have unpaid bills, you will march at graduation with cap and gown and receive an empty folder on stage, with the degree available to you only after the bills are paid. In this case, you have earned, but do not have, a bachelor's degree.

Unpaid college loans may not be factored into bankruptcies. Often, holders of private loans cannot afford to serve in the Peace Corps, since repayment rates are not adjusted to income.

Books and articles have chronicled these events over the past twenty years; some intellectuals manage even now not to be aware of them or to attribute them to "the cultural issues of those who cannot pay."

We are all complicit; collectively we've lost control.

Citing these figures is sometimes wrongly interpreted as bellyaching on the part of underpaid instructors. That is a diversion. The real victims are students, who are told they will get nowhere without the degree. The parents, similarly, are terrified that others' children may get the advantage over their own. Conservative commercial weekly Forbes says that, even so, sixty percent of college graduates today do not find work in their field.

The money lenders in these schemes will carry on as long as permitted, maybe not forever. If you didn't have available the facts above, then shame on the instigators and their boards of directors. If you did, and accepted them, then shame on you. There would be a third option, but so far the fearful crawl into the bushes. As we know, when running with a friend from an attacking bear, you need not run fast. Just faster than your friend.

Linear Thinking
August 28, 2016

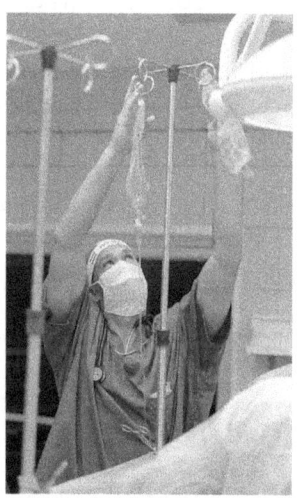

It's a well-known fact that 64.7 per cent of American physicians spend late August on Martha's Vineyard, and deserve to. You knew that, but may not know that this year, the percentage unexplainably reached a record 82.4 per cent, causing increased pressure on the island's fragile ecosystem and referring added weight to the ocean floor. This in turn indirectly caused the recent calamity in Italy, severely damaging the beautiful towns of Amatrice and Piscaro del Tronto, and causing tremors as far away as Myanmar on the same day, August 24.

The indisputable source of this information is a new scientific method making the rounds in the U.S. presidential elections: *someone said so*. You may think Candidate Trump is original in this line of reasoning. But the Dalai Lama predated him by at least fourteen years, citing it in his discourse to 3,000 listeners at the U.S. National Cathedral on the second anniversary of the terrorist attacks of 9/11. Here is a link to the transcript.
https://www.savetibet.org/dalai-lama-stresses-long-term-peaceful-measures-to-prevent-recurrence-of-911-tragedy/

I love His Holiness the Fourteenth for many things, but not for his linear thinking. I am also grateful he does not seek to be president of the United States.

Here is my point, and I want to put it out before the memory fades: the food poisoning occurred Sunday, August 21. By Monday, I understood that the symptoms weren't related to food poisoning after all. I began to suspect kidney stones. I went to an emergency room at 9:30 p.m. I won't say which hospital because I can't afford a lawyer.

They asked me the reason for my visit. I said, "Fever, vomiting, localized and general pain, nausea, and something strange in my urine. Maybe it's kidney stones."

"Ah," they said. "Let's have a look. It could be kidney stones." Good thinking.

At midnight, the reasoning shifted to cancer. Well, maybe no catheter, in that case.

After two CT scans, by 2:00am the working theory changed to kidney cyst. I was on a very enabling drip and passed through these three different phases oh so sweetly.

The ER discharged me at 4:50am August 23, with written orders to have a follow-up with a urologist preferably within 24 hours, but no later than 48 hours from my time of discharge. The orders included the phone numbers of two urologists, one of them on the staff of the hospital.

Damn, I thought. If I'd gone in during working hours, I might have seen one quicker.

The next day from home I lifted my gravity-challenged head and dialed the numbers, both of them incorrect. Not even close, *not even the correct area code*. I phoned around to numbers posted on the Urology-R-Us website, taking in two states and a district, the DMV (the Washington DC metropolitan area).

No urologists around. They were mostly on Martha's Vineyard as noted, a few others in game parks and some at beaches and pubs. But Urology-R-Us did have correct phone numbers for the docs on my discharge papers. I called them, one office I counted 22 times. No answering device. A receptionist did pick up the 23rd call, and I got an appointment eleven days from the time of ER discharge. I took it gladly, but kept looking. Being a patient in DC is very competitive and demanding. Only the best succeed.

I used the word "cancer" a few times for emphasis in the following dozen calls, but it didn't work. What they wanted to hear was, "Maybe sometime in mid to late September."

I landed a physician referral service in northern Virginia. The desk said, "Here are three names, but they are all in pediatrics. Is that a problem for you?"

I said, "Not at all, just so you know I haven't been a child for some decades. I hope they deal with kidney issues."

"No problem, sir, they can surely do that. Here are three."

I wrote them down and said, "So they are all in pediatrics?"

She answered, "No, none of them."

"Sorry for asking," I said.

Reader, you have been through this sort of thing and know I am not making any of this up, except maybe "Urology-R-Us."

I got an appointment from another service for August 25, the third day of my ER discharge. Not with an MD, but a nurse practitioner. The referral service said, "Will this be ok?"

"Absolutely," I said. "Nurse practitioner. Great."

I saw the nurse Thursday morning. She asked, "Is there any pain? There shouldn't be."

"There is," I said. "Right here."

"There shouldn't be," she countered.

"Then I'm wondering why did I go to the emergency room Monday night?"

"You did the right thing. No pain, right?"

"Right," I said. "I must have been mistaken."

At that point an MD stepped in, tall, melancholic man with a drooping moustache.

"I'm glad to meet you, Doctor. The ER said kidney stones, then cancer, then cyst."

"Don't interrupt," the doctor said. I would have apologized, but it would have been another interruption. "It's a cyst on the kidney, 5.5cm," he said. "There shouldn't be any pain."

"Very grateful," I said, figuring with my thumb and finger what must have been 5.5 cm, about three inches. I thought: *Alien, the Remake*.

"Is that kind of big?" I asked.

"We've seen bigger," he said.

"Is it possible anything might go wrong?" I asked.

"It's possible," he said.

"Then what?" I said.

"Then go back to the emergency room."

I am not at all seeking to ding the so-called "broken medical system" in the United States. If there is such a thing, it's not because of Obamacare or socialized medicine or single payer or vigilante justice or whatever you want to blame. It's because there lacks linear thinking in our country at this time. The same happens with power companies, banks, universities, condos, schools, phones, gravel spreaders, and kitchen supplies, as we all know.

Here is my point: people are not getting oxygen to their brain, and need to fix this. Kundalini or HathaYoga, TM, candle flames, longer vacations, or maybe just deep breathing. The oxygen isn't getting there. It's a well-known fact. Somebody said so.

You can't be wrong all the time, and maybe one talking point merits consideration: America could lose its greatness if we aren't vigilant. People should inhale more (air) and very urgently, and concentrate on fewer things at once; then there could be hope. But toot sweet, before it's too late.

If not, then probably not.

Village Fool
August 29, 2016

'Ti Laurent wasn't right in the head, and wandered from footpath to footpath saying, *"Tu fais bien, c'est pour toi; tu fais mal, c'est pour toi."* ["When you do good, it's on you; when you do bad, it's on you." "What goes around comes around."]

He didn't have much of a repertoire, and depended on the kindness of others. The village took him in, because it was their culture to do so.

"Tu fais bien, c'est pour toi;

Tu fais mal, c'est pour toi."

People heard his relentless message and took it as part of the ambient sounds, like the rooster announcing sun up or the brook tonguing the pebbles beneath, during the rainy season.

Mama Prisca had six children. She put up with 'Ti Laurent not because she wanted to, but because that was the way of the village. Everyone gave him handouts but no one really wanted him around. He was weird. No one knew if he would lash out at children if his spring ever came loose.

'Ti Laurent came by most mornings, and Mama Prisca gave him any leftovers from the kids' school lunch. There wasn't much choice about it. She didn't have much extra, but hoarding was not acceptable in the village. She had given up long ago trying to say anything to him or get any words other than

"Tu fais bien, c'est pour toi;

Tu fais mal, c'est pour toi."

Others helped, but Mama Prisca took most of the burden because she was first on his morning rounds.

Tuesday she got her children ready – the four older ones to school, the other two at home. 'Ti Laurent came by for his usual handout. Suddenly he grabbed for Anice, and Mama Prisca pulled her away from him to safety. Anice was four. There was no telling what he was after. He had a demon's face just for a moment, but probably didn't mean anything by it.

Wednesday Mama Prisca decided she had had enough, realized there was no hospital, no social services (dream on), no constabulary to take care of such things. She was not in favor of vigilante justice, but her maternal juices flowed. It was easy enough to make poison from the leaves of the calabo and ceiba trees, mixed with some dust from the Chinese aphrodisiac in the market. The local sages and healers might not know the chemical compound, but trial and error had proven it effective. The community would lose nothing if 'Ti Laurent were removed from the equation. Something had to give life predictability.

The next day Mama Prisca put poison in the ground cassava root she gave to 'Ti Laurent. He took it and left with a disdainful thank you, as always.

'Ti Laurent got distracted that day, and went to the stream to watch the water flow over the pebbles. If he was hungry he forgot. He celebrated the freedom of being an eccentric, and walked the length and breadth of the village, glad that unlike the others, he had no obligations.

He lingered by the stream until afternoon when the children walked home from school. They knew him and said hi as they always did. He offered them the ground cassava root Mama Prisca had given him. They ate hungrily and gratefully.

When the four children returned home they had horrible stomach aches, and Mama Prisca was very alarmed. They wailed with discomfort and vomited on their bed. Mama Prisca asked why this was happening.

"We ate cassava from 'Ti Laurent. He gave it to us," Lamou, the eight-year-old son, said.

Mama Prisca howled with panic and tried to make a powder cure for the poison in the ground cassava root, but she couldn't remember the ingredients. She went through the neighborhood asking if anyone could help. She wailed and cried and had the greatest anguish. She came from her neighbor Lore and rushed home with some ideas for a cure, but it was too late; all four children were dead. She rocked with agony and cursed god. It was unfair, unequal, unjust, and a cruel joke for this to happen. She wailed all night and the neighbors came to comfort her and her two surviving toddlers, who had not much understanding of what was happening.

'Ti Laurent came to the door in the morning, unaware of what had happened. He came as he often did, to find out if Mama Prisca had anything extra for him for the day.

"Go to hell and I hope your bones rot!" she said. "The tsetse fly will bite your penis until it drops off, idiot-monster," she added.

He looked at her with puzzlement, not able to articulate his confusion or innocence.

"The food I gave you yesterday, my children! All four, dead!" Mama Prisca said, still wailing from the night before.

'Ti Laurent said,

"Tu fais bien, c'est pour toi;

Tu fais mal, c'est pour toi."

He shrugged and walked away.

www.ingramcontent.com/pod-product-compliance
Lightning Source LLC
Chambersburg PA
CBHW020750160426
43192CB00006B/287